TABLE OF CONTENTS

Preface	2
January 12, 2012	9
Refugees of Fear	31
Taking Steps	51
Jacmel	65
God in the Corner	79
The Cave	95
Strangers and Brothers	107
Satan in the Streets	121
Meeting Jesus	139
Something Strange in the Air	155
Piecing Life Together	167
Alphabet Soup	181
Distraction Therapy	195
Aftershocks in our Minds	211

PREFACE

When two English speaking non Haitians sit next to each other on the flight to Port-au-Prince, the conversation between them usually goes something like this:

"So, what are you going to Haiti for?" One curious Caucasian leans over slightly and asks the obligatory question.

-"Mission work, orphanage, relief, education programs, deal drugs…" One of these usual responses is returned.

"Is this your first time to Haiti?"

-"Yes, I'm really excited but kind of nervous." or "I've been going down every year for so many years."

"What part of Haiti are you going to?"

-"I don't know if I'm pronouncing it right, but…" or "Out in the mountains a place called…" or "Port-au-Prince." Usually Port-au-Prince.

Lee Rainboth
3/5/14

THE GRINDER

ONE COMMUNITY'S JOURNEY THROUGH PAIN AND HOPE
FROM THE GREAT HAITI EARTHQUAKE

LEE RAINBOTH

"Well that's really great!"

-"Thanks." And then they go back to eating their pretzels.

Here's how it goes for me:

"So, what are you going to Haiti for?"

-"I live down there."

"Oh really, how long have you been living there?"

-"For about 6 years now."

"Oh. Oh… so… were you there for the…" They lean into the silence unsure if they should actually say the word.

-"Earthquake? Yeah." They slowly set their pretzels down.

"Wow…" They squint and look at my face to see if they heard me right. "Really? So… what was that like?"

At this point I usually respond with some one word answer that will hopefully cut the conversation off, "Horrifying, traumatic, unforgettable." Or, if I'm in a good mood, I just switch the conversation back to them and ask about whatever projects they intend to help out with once they get to Haiti. I do this because I know that the story is so deep and complex that I can't pretend to do it justice on the short ride to Port-au-Prince. Sometimes I'll tell them that someday I'll have a book published and they can read the full story then.

When people find out that I survived the earthquake they seldom know how to react. Most of them coming to Haiti probably were inspired to do so because of the earthquake and find it hard to believe that there were any foreigners involved in the country before that. It's easy to assume that people that look similar to ourselves and come from a similar geographic origin probably have a similar story to our own. We expect the survivor stories to come from people who look like the Haitians that we saw on the news in those days following the quake and we don't expect their stories to have anything in common with our own. Because they exist on the other side of the lines that we draw between the people needing help and the people who can provide help. And somehow life is easier to muddle through when all the people on each side of that line have one huge generalized story for each other. That's when it's clear what pronouns we are supposed to use, "us" and "them".

But when we take the time to hear just one individual story that line starts to fade because we are invited to participate in their story with them. And with each additional story that is told and heard, the lines fade more and more until they are not even noticeable any longer.

This book is that invitation to participate in the story. Not only my own story of what I lived through during the earthquake in Haiti of January 12, 2010, but the story of my community that lived through it with me. That community is Mizak, a rural area near Jacmel on the southern coast, miles away from Port-au-Prince and the devastation that was seen on the news reports all over the world in the days after the quake. Mizak, however, and those who live there, was not far removed from the tragedy that was born from that quake. The people in this community felt the effects of the quake in a very different way than those in the capitol, but none less significantly, and this book is my way to share their side of the story.

The stories represented in this book were collected in the months following the earthquake as a project of Living Media International as a sort of therapy through creative expression. It was a way to remind each other of the beauty that remained in life. Early on after the quake all anyone could see was the ugly. Through allowing them the opportunity to sit down and share their stories and get them down in writing we could also push them to look for where the hope would lie farther ahead. In the casual conversations with neighbors as everyone would tell what they had lived it was easy to focus on all the bad things that had occurred. By structuring people's story telling with a more concrete goal in mind and in an environment of support and understanding, then they could process the fears more effectively and begin to see beyond them.

No names have been changed as those involved wanted their stories to be shared in their truest forms possible and all agreed to having them included in the book. To some this book was their only hope of having their voices heard.

I am fortunate to be considered a part of this community and am honored that they would trust me with their stories in this way. At the time of writing this it has been six years since I moved to Mizak. I was drawn to the area because of the work of a specific organization that was centered there, Haitian Artisans for Peace International (HAPI). I was invited to work with them because of my experience as an artist to assist their women's fair trade cooperative in the areas of product development and quality control. I had previously worked with other artisan groups and nonprofits in Mali, Uganda, and Kenya, so the opportunity intrigued me. The original decision to spend six months in Haiti was mostly an experiment, a stamp to add to my passport that wasn't African. I looked forward to learning about a new culture closer to home but never expected to become part of that culture.

I soon learned that Haiti existed as a contradiction to all expectations. Two and a half years later, just months before the earthquake, I was building my own home, building my own organization, and building a new life that looked more and more like it belonged in this country.

After the time that I had spent, although I was ready for change, I couldn't possibly leave that community that I had been absorbed into. Even though I had fulfilled my duty to the artisans' coop, I had developed a new duty to my peers in the community who were thirsty for opportunities to make a difference. They are the ones who persuaded me to stick around and helped lay the groundwork for what would become Living Media International. I knew beyond all doubt that I was meant to be there. Yet, it wasn't until the earthquake struck and sent us all into the same state of fear and uncertainty regardless of our race, class, or background, that I fully discovered the power that exists in belonging to such a community. It is that hope that I don't believe would be found in other more individualized cultures that the stories in this book, speaking together, are meant to illuminate.

Although through these stories many issues are explored such as humanitarian aid, religion, and racial identity, the intent is not to analyze such issues to arrive at any conclusion but simply to show their role in the big picture of the event. As noted throughout the book my conclusion is that enough words have already been hurled at the country and at the situation caused by the disaster to try to provide reasons for it all, but they only make things more confounding in the end. We can forever continue to ask why and try to explain something that's not meant to be explained, but the only real way to step forward towards a different future is to begin to understand each other a little more completely. That is what can happen through our stories.

By reading on in this book, you not only are agreeing to open your eyes to a different perspective and see what it's like in someone else's shoes, but you are agreeing to help carry the load of those who must walk in those shoes daily. By reading you are sending a message that their stories have value and their struggles will not be forgotten. Although you, the reader, may never meet any of these individuals who are represented by the stories in this book, by turning the page you are stepping into their community and walking alongside them as they push forward toward a future worth surviving for.

Men anpil, chay pa lou.

Many hands make the load lighter.

-Haitian proverb

ARTWORK BY LEE RAINBOTH

JANUARY 12, 2010

Haitians believe that anytime you see a falling star shoot through the sky, it signifies somebody's death. Because from the moment of conception in their mother's womb, every human being has a star appear for them. Then all through their life they have this star shining for them, reminding them that they're still alive. The really bright stars represent the wealthiest and most powerful people while the many fainter ones that you have to squint to see even on the clearest of nights belong to the poor and weak. But then when it is time for a person to leave their life in this world behind, then it is time for their star to leave its place in the sky so it goes shooting off in the direction of the place where that person will die. This is why many Haitians are afraid to see falling stars and if they happen to catch a glimpse of one, they may run and hide inside because they don't want to be the one to die.

When I would hear my Haitian friends say these things I used to joke around with them about being so superstitious and then try to teach them astronomy, as if that even mattered in the face of their cultural beliefs. As if I was an expert after my one class I took in college to fulfill a science requirement.

Then the earthquake hit.

And on that night as I lay on my back on the rocky ground just a few yards away from the ruins of the house that I was so proud of building, along with all of the other neighbors who were afraid to stay in their cracked and damaged houses, all bundled up, in the few sheets and sweatshirts that they could find, I stared up into the night sky and saw more falling stars than I've ever seen before. Within minutes of lying down, I had lost count. My Astronomy 101 class would have told me there was a meteor shower. My gut told me that the Haitian superstitions weren't so silly. Lying there, I had no idea how many people actually died from the earthquake that day, but I know what I saw in that sky. The image of the trails of star after star running to their deaths across the vast darkness of that Haitian night will forever remain etched in my mind as the image of January 12, 2010. As I watched the stars fall one after another, I reflected on a day that still seemed like a dream.

It began just like any other day, not presenting any reason to remember it past the 13th. That morning I spent some time working at the HAPI medical clinic. I had moved on to check on the construction site of my new home where the workers kept making things look better and better. My mom had sent extra money for the construction work, and my good friend and project manager, Papi, used it to buy more materials for tasks at hand. And that was that. In the afternoon I went back to the HAPI guesthouse where I showered, got dressed, then went outside to sit on the little wall with my roommate and photography student, Sony, to teach him how to use the self-timer on his camera.

It was about 5:00 when it happened.

I grabbed Sony's knee and he grabbed mine as the earth shook beneath us. Neither of us had ever experienced an earthquake but we recognized what it was. We both just sort of sat there, stunned, and looked at each other puzzled, hoping to find some explanation for this wonder in the other's face. We were two people of different ages and races, from completely different cultures and backgrounds, but at that moment we reflected each other's confusion as two humans caught together in a single, inconceivable event. We probably should have gotten up and away from the wall that we were leaning against but we didn't know what to do. All that I could do was sit there in solitude with Sony, searching for reasons that neither of us knew, and wait for it to be over. We heard something crash and shatter inside the house, and then, several seconds later, stillness.

* * *

It was August 2007 and I sat on another small wall next to Sony Gere. This wall was in front of his aunt's house. His aunt was married to the director of Haitian Artisans for Peace International (HAPI), Paul, and I had just entered the country less than a week earlier to work for his organization. I had graduated from college at Iowa State University just a few months earlier and had decided to move to Haiti more or less on a whim after having received an email from a friend telling me about HAPI. I had never expected I would move to Haiti after having done extensive traveling in Africa; I always thought I would end up back there. But after reading that email, something inside me whispered, "What the hell, go for it," so I decided to follow up and give the whole Haiti thing a try.

At that point I knew exactly two things about Haiti. First, I knew the cliché that the entire world knows about Haiti, which is that it is the poorest country in the Western Hemisphere. After that, I knew that the country did house some incredible artistic talent. I had a great uncle who had lived in Haiti for some time working for an orphanage years before. Although none of the family really knew much about his work there, after his death, they held on to his extensive collection of diverse Haitian art. Through this art, I was able to learn quite a bit about the country. I knew what the colorful markets looked like and what kind of products the people sold there. I could imagine the intense activity that occurs at a Haitian cockfight. I could also envision the cities with their historic architecture. That all was enough to draw me there. I signed up for an original stint of six months volunteering for HAPI.

When I first arrived, it was Paul and his family that hosted me in their own home and within a matter of days from arriving, their nephew, Sony, had discovered me. In the evenings when the family was preparing dinner I would go outside and sit on the small wall in their front yard to write in my journal and enjoy the peacefulness of the Haitian countryside. Once Sony found me he made it his mission to disrupt that peacefulness. He was 15-years-old at the time and would come over nightly to sit with me on the wall, his feet dangling unable to reach the ground, and speak Creole at me while laughing at the blank looks that it brought to my face. He would try to teach me, but would lose patience quickly and just resort to petting my head and smiling instead. Once I really got to know Sony I realized that the whole time he was speaking Creole he was probably insulting me, but it didn't matter. From the start I recognized Sony as innocently obnoxious. He was bold and friendly, but even through the language barrier, I could tell a bit rude. He was just annoying enough for me to love like the little brother that I never had.

He soon began leading his younger siblings, Joslyn and Berline, over to talk at and pet this tall white man that was hanging out at their aunt's house. In this rural Haitian community with no electricity, running water, or finished roads, it seemed at the time that petting a white man was the most entertaining thing they could find to do with their time. I eventually started picking up on vocabulary and finding the ability to communicate simply with these children. By the time that I had perfected the use of some of the most basic words, "to come" and "house", Sony wasted no time in giving me the chance to practice them as he invited me to his home to meet his family.

When I responded with an enthusiastic "wi" he and Berline led me to their nearby home. It was a typical Haitian home built of concrete blocks with a rusted tin roof and consisted of four small rooms with bright heart designs painted on the outside in Pepto Bismol-pink. Sitting outside was their mother Julie, a short, cheerful looking lady with very light skin looking more Central American than Haitian. With her were 11-year-old Joslyn, whom I knew already, Theodore, who was one year older than Sony, Berthony, older brother Nicodem, sister Pascale, and cousin, Majorie, who looked about my age. Julie and the entire family greeted me warmly and gave me a chair to sit with them all in the courtyard of their small house. They explained to me that their father, Bebe was out in the field, and they also had two older siblings who lived in Port-au-Prince, making a grand total of nine kids, two parents, plus Majorie who had been adopted into the family. Then they were quick to clarify that I now made the thirteenth member of the family. Apparently Sony had been telling them quite a bit about me and they were all looking forward to meeting me.

I too was filled with gratitude for having met them. I remember thinking from that first night how appropriate those silly pink hearts were on the outside of their home because it was clearly a home filled with love beyond what I had seen in other Haitian homes. I knew immediately that I would become good friends with this family. I had been hoping to make more friends close to my age in the community and celebrated meeting Sony's older siblings. Berthony was 19 then and he especially proved to be a good time to be around from the start. He had a smile full of the straightest, whitest teeth that I had seen in Haiti, and a laugh that convinced me from the day that I met him that we would get along well.

After meeting at their home, Berthony and Sony began coming over to Paul's house every night to keep teaching me Creole and play the Haitian card game, casino, with me. They would come over every evening after dinner, say hello to their aunt to be polite, then come straight into my room and start shuffling the deck of cards. I can't say that I completely enjoyed casino. It involved too much math for this artist, but I enjoyed the boys' company so much that I didn't mind playing along. When we got tired of playing, we would always put the cards away and just lay on the bed speaking in Creole. It was in those moments that I learned. With the help of those two I was becoming fluent within a matter of a couple months. Those first six months that I spent in Haiti, Sony and Berthony were there every night until I left, without fail, to play casino and speak Creole.

As I continued to return to Haiti to work with HAPI, and decided to stay long term, I eventually moved into the small guesthouse owned by HAPI. Having decided that life is simply more enjoyable when lived with other human beings, I invited my two new best friends, Sony and Berthony, to stay there with me. A fourth roommate, my other good friend, and another cousin of the boys, Papi, joined us as well there in what soon became known as "Baz Bukson" meaning the Bachelor Base.

Papi was the old man of our Baz Bukson and possessed the maturity and laid back attitude to balance Sony's abrasive youth. He was the first friend that I made when I came to Haiti. He was there when I arrived at his cousin, Paul's, house and he was the one to unload my luggage from the truck to put in my room. Since then he's never stopped being the most helpful person I know. No matter what I need, he's always there by my side to share the load, not just physically, but also as a reliable source of advice and friendship.

The time that I spent living together in this house with these three young men transformed my relationship with them beyond simple friendship and into brotherhood. They are the ones who actually made life enjoyable enough to live in this country that I was able to continue deciding to stick around.

I had stuck around for two and a half years when I decided to make a change, leaving HAPI and starting a new organization with different focus, which also meant I would need to build my own home. I had also come to deeply care for my new found family there and my peers in the community and could not just leave them even if I decided to leave HAPI.

Transition was already ruling my life on that fateful day that we all lost stability. If you had asked me three years earlier where I would be on January 12, 2010, I would have never dreamed to have responded, "Haiti".

* * *

The stillness lasted only for a brief moment for everyone to confirm that the earthquake had indeed passed. Then, the cries began coming from all directions, "Anmwey![1]" "Seigneur Jezi![2]" "Oh Bondye[3]!" Sony and I broke our gaze from each other and went inside to find that the mirror had fallen off the wall and broken into pieces on the floor. After that everything seemed to be okay at the house, so we cleaned up

---

[1] A Creole cry of distress without translation
[2] Lord Jesus
[3] Oh God

the mess, collected our things, and headed out.

Based on what we had seen, we had no reason to believe that the event was significant or terrible, because we had no experience to compare it to and all that it broke was our mirror. So we left the house lighthearted and laughing, thinking that all the people we heard yelling to God were silly for being so scared. As we walked out into the community, the first few neighbors houses that we passed didn't give us any reason to believe otherwise either. They all seemed to be in normal condition with smiling people out front. It wasn't until we began approaching the site of my new house that we began to realize that something wasn't right. As we climbed the small mountain to my house we saw a crowd of people standing all around it shaking their heads, pointing to different parts of the building, and talking to each other. As we got closer we passed a small group of several other people sitting on the rocks nearby in silence with their backs to the house, seeming unwilling to look at it at all. That's where I noticed Berthony, and the look on his face told me that we weren't going to like what we were about to see.

Everything was on schedule and looking like we were going to be able to move into the house by February 1st as planned. All that remained to finish on the house was putting on the doors and windows, installing the tile floor, and a few decorative details. As an artist I had ensured that every detail contributed to designing a building that would be beautiful. And those building the home were artists themselves continually surprising me with the elements they would add, especially my contractor, Junior, whose creativity directed the outcome of the work.

The whole community had been following the progress of my home construction to see how things changed each day to become more and more fantastic. Now, it seemed that as soon as the ground stilled on the 12th, many in the community had run to my house first, to see if it was still standing. That was the crowd that we saw there on my hilltop as Sony and I approached the house.

When I saw the defeat in Berthony's expression as we passed by, I wasn't sure that I wanted to continue. I knew how serious a situation had to be in order to erase the smile from Berthony's face. I didn't know if I wanted to look.

My heart sank as we got closer and began to see the damage. It was as if God took the roof and just gave it a huge shove to the east, shifting it several feet and breaking all the walls underneath of it in the process. It was still standing thanks to the temporary steel support beams that were used to hold up the wooden framework that was created to give the shape of the roof, but it was clear that the house was ruined. We made the 360° walk around the house to arrive next to Boss Junior out front in the crowd of people. You could tell that he was just as sick as I was to see his masterpiece trashed. He confirmed my fear that there really was nothing left to salvage besides the foundation and we would have to start completely over. It was a finished house. Now, in a brief moment, it was all laid to waste.

As I stood there staring, dumbfounded, studying every little crack, I realized that my primary disappointment was not at the loss of the house. Yes, it was a lot of time and money down the drain and it hurt to see something so beautiful get destroyed, but it's just cement and, in time, I knew we'd be able to find the money to rebuild. I was aware of the privilege that I possessed being American that offered me the assurance of rebuilding that my Haitian neighbors were not so lucky to have. My ethnicity gave me the faith that it was not quite a dream deferred, just postponed. However, I knew that there were some people in this world who would take pleasure in my loss, and that's what really upset me. Although I knew that I had the support of the majority of the people in this community, there were still some who had been jealous, not so much of the house itself, but of the fact that I didn't choose to build it on their land, or hire them for labor, or buy sand from them, and so on. They're jealous that they weren't able to make any money off of the white man.

In the states there were those people who thought I wasn't making the right decision to build a house here and to stay in this community and people who were jealous in their own way that I was able to make those decisions. And now all of these people would be laughing at me, or saying that I deserved it somehow, or saying that it was some sort of message that I was supposed to learn from. I felt at that point that I wasn't just looking at crumbling walls but I was looking at the pettiness of the human race, and that was the most frustrating part of all. Berthony later said, "Mouths broke this house." God or Mother Nature or physics may have played roles in breaking my house, but the critics and doubters and jealous ones with their negative words paved the way.

Perhaps no one knew this better than Papi. As the most trustworthy and hard-working individual that I knew, he was the obvious choice to coordinate the entire construction process for me when we started the house. I also knew how heavy of a burden that responsibility would be and I knew that if anyone could handle it, it was Papi. He endured a lot of criticism and harassment from others through the process. They would say that he was an idiot for doing a white man's work and not making any money off it. They would say that I was an idiot for choosing such an uneducated, inexperienced man to facilitate such a task. They would question him relentlessly when I would give him money to buy materials, or when I would have him receive a transfer from the states to pay the workers. At multiple points I actually had to talk Papi out of moving to the Dominican Republic when he was so discouraged and ready to just leave all the mouths behind where he couldn't hear their malicious babble.

But it was difficult for me to tell him to stay when I knew how cruel society could be. I didn't want him having to suffer such degradation either. Sometimes it felt like maybe the best solution would have been for us all to just run away. But we didn't because I was confident of my place there, at that moment after the quake more than ever. Also, more than anything, I like a challenge. So we decided to rebuild and move on, knowing that my baz would be there with me through it all. It just took a little time to figure out exactly how we would move on. Disaster insurance on your home isn't really an option in Mizak so we knew that the only way we would be able to move on was to rest on complete faith.

Ultimately, as everyone had been saying, we really did all have to be very thankful that no one got hurt at the house. The construction workers were on the site, cleaning up from the day's work, when the quake hit. Some were even inside the house, but were able to get out and away before pieces started falling. Many friends who live nearby, as well as myself, had even been enjoying ourselves up on the rooftop in the afternoons ever since it got finished. It was the perfect place to take in the fresh mountain breeze and marvel at the extraordinary view, but on that afternoon, at that pivotal moment, we all happened to be elsewhere and no one was on top of the house. If anyone had been, it would have surely been far more tragic than it already was.

* * *

I sat on the ledge of the foundation of the HAPI clinic and started to daydream. I had been in this community for two years and was trying to make decisions for the future. Here I sat alone.

I had started looking around the community for houses to buy or even rent to live in, but couldn't find any. It was while working at the clinic that I would sit there on the porch and look off to the northeast at a small hilltop and start to think of a different possibility. Berthony and his friends would frequently congregate on the rocks that covered the hill in the afternoons to study their school lessons and I had made a habit of sitting with them to write in my journal. I knew how gorgeous the view was from there and how inspirational it was feeling a little like you were on top of the world. If you stood on top of the hill and looked downward to the north you could see the public school and the radio station and the central market just behind them with the neighbors' avocado and tangerine trees all scattered in between. If you look off in the distance to the north you can see the mountain range that sits in between Port-au-Prince and us. It's that mountain range that you have to wind through up and down and back and forth for three hours by car to get to the capitol from Mizak. If you look off to the south you can see another mountain range in the distance and just beyond that is the Caribbean. From that vantage point, if you know the right mountain peaks to look between at the right time of day, you can actually see the sea in its brilliant turquoise blue color as it melts into the sky at the horizon. There was only one tree on the hilltop, after that nothing but a beautiful, open space just begging to have a house built on it. There were fields of corn and brown beans planted from the foot of the hill about halfway up, but the top was too rocky to grow anything, and so it remained bare, a blank canvas for my imagination to wander.

I would find myself in front of the clinic, closing my eyes and picturing what my house would look like up there. I kept my visions to myself, however, knowing a thousand reasons why such an idea wouldn't be realistic. I had plenty of people back home reminding me that such ideas weren't realistic from the start. There were plenty of people seeming to think that I'd probably had my fun in Haiti by then and didn't really need to be thinking about buying, renting, or building any home in such a place. What I had done while I was there was honorable and all, in their eyes, but they made it clear that they thought it was time to get back to the real world and do something more serious with my life. I could only play humanitarian for so long. If I was going to stay in Haiti, it wasn't realistic to believe that I could just go off and do it on my own. And yet, my experience in Haiti so far had taught me that the least realistic seeming idea would probably be the one that would end up becoming reality. "What the hell, go for it," I would hear the whisper tempting my renegade soul.

I eventually mentioned the wild idea to Berthony and Sony and they agreed with me. They had always thought that a beautiful house belonged up there on that hilltop. Conveniently, their father, Bebe, owned the land, so they talked to him about it, and soon enough, we were signing the papers and breaking ground. We started the countdown to moving in knowing that if we stayed on schedule the house would be ready for us by the beginning of February.

*　*　*

It was while we stood there in the crowd gathered before my house that we began to hear reports of damage to other homes and the effects of the disaster in other areas. One neighbor's roof split down the center and kitchen had completely toppled. Another neighboring family had two houses both fallen flat on the earth. Sacre Coeur Church roof was severed with the bell tower had collapsed... piece by piece the reality of the disaster was setting in. People came and went and flowed through the community touring the aftermath, and talking about God a lot. They would say things like, "It's the work of God, there's nothing we can do," "God's an old man and He does what He likes," and, "All we can do is praise God that we're still alive." But then the news began trickling in that not everybody had made it through alive, and people were catching information on their radios of how far the devastation spread. Jacmel, Tomb Gateau, Leogane... Port-au-Prince.

Berthony and I decided to enter the flow of people milling about. We couldn't sit there in front of the house anymore. We decided to go check on Paul and his family. When we arrived on their porch we found the family gathered around the radio listening to a CNN report in English. I pulled up a chair by the radio and started listening intently to see what news was coming in from other parts. Berthony, however, would not even go near any walls or sit under the tin roof covering the porch. He went out and sat on the grass in the front yard by himself instead. He pulled his knees up against his chest and hugged them tightly grasping for some sense of security.

It was from that radio report that I started to really understand the situation in Port-au-Prince. "All you can see when you look at the city is a cloud of dust," the reporter said. After that it turned into a geography lesson of the capitol without many details on the actual situation on hand. The reporter's attitude towards the Haitians was irritating, as if they are all violent, murderous thieves who would take advantage of the situation to create more chaos. It may have been true that crime would actually be a big problem after this, but she was painting broad generalizations that didn't shed any light on what was truly happening. So I didn't listen for long and quit straining to hear through the static, but I had heard enough to know that the city was demolished.

What the Haitians were hearing on the radio was to not enter their houses and to certainly not sleep in their houses because the aftershock tremors would continue for a while and no one knew what would happen after all the walls were weakened in the original quake. So we had to decide what we were going to do for the night.

It had gotten dark while we were at Paul's and several strong tremors had occurred, so we went by my house and literally ran in to grab some sheets and blankets and ran back out to then search for a place to sleep for the night. Our search brought us to the rocks under the stars near my ruined house. Several other families had already camped out there so we found a relatively flat spot in amongst them and settled down. Berthony wedged himself into a small crack between his best friend Petuel and myself. He pulled a sheet up over his head and tried to escape from the world that was falling apart around him. He was trembling and terrified. Ever since I found him earlier he hadn't been himself. He hadn't been speaking. My heart ached to see his smile fade and disappear. I didn't know what to do for him. I just lay close to him, letting him know I was there, and rolled over on my back allowing my eyes to wander up into the sky. The first star fell into my eye and turned into a tear.

Someone shouted out, "You see how close of neighbors you have here, Lee?" There in our little camp, the interconnectedness of the community began to reveal that although this tragedy was horrible and heartbreaking, there was also something strangely wonderful in what was happening among the survivors. They were all united in having experienced the same tragedy and they all shared in each other's pain. I was humbly overwhelmed to be a part of it. Where I come from we expect to see these things on the news from the comfort of our living rooms, but there I was, lying on the rocks with my neighbors, a part of the story. It was clear that that was the only way that we would all be able to ever move on - together. It was in those moments in the hours following the quake that the true depth of the Haitian spirit began to awake and expose itself.

It was true that people could be petty and hate on you until your house breaks, but as soon as they realize that the tragedy has hit them too, they forget about whether or not you rented their cistern to hold water for your construction. In that moment when people began lying together on the earth that God sculpted underneath of them, the material things of buildings and money and possessions didn't matter like they did yesterday. All that mattered was that you were alive and any conflicts you may have had with your neighbor were forgotten. It's impossible to hold a grudge in your heart against someone who may have just lost his or her child or his or her spouse or his or her parent without even knowing it yet. And at that moment that could have been any of us. None of us knew anything. All we knew was what we saw before us so we had to be thankful for the people that were alive around us to exist by our side in those troubling moments, no matter who they were.

Sony passed by with a few other friends and told us about other camps that had sprung up around the community. They had deemed themselves the community's ad hoc news reporters and were making the rounds telling everyone of the situation. 30 people here, 100 at the top of the market, 70 by the voodoo parastile, and many more up by Sacre Coeur. So, after a couple hours with our neighbors but unable to fall asleep, I went with Berthony and Petuel to check out some of the more populated bases. We ended up in the market where someone had laid out a huge white tarp that was covered with people literally lying on top of each other. We stayed here until morning, weaving ourselves into the pile of refugees.

Cell phone communication had been cut off since the quake, but that didn't stop everyone from trying. Everyone wanted to know if their families in other parts of the country were okay or not, but no one could get through on the phone. We all just had to rely on what we heard on the radio and leave the rest up to some higher power. Despite the reality that absolutely no one was getting through on their phones, I kept trying desperately on mine as well to reach my mother in the states. For hours I had no luck just like everyone else but when we arrived there on the tarp at the market, about 11:00 at night, I gave her one last try and by some miracle, I got through. The connection wasn't clear so I cried, "I'm okay, but the house is destroyed. I'm okay." I prayed that she heard me. I could hear her voice saying that they saw the news and had been very worried, but it was clear that she was having trouble hearing me respond. "I'm okay," I repeated. "I'm okay. My brothers here are okay." I tried to say more, explaining what we were going through, but the call got cut.

After that I could relax a little. I had no idea how much she heard, but at least she knew I was alive. I wove myself back into the tapestry of refugees. I can't say that any of us slept because the tremors kept coming every half hour or so and each time one hit everyone would start screaming to Jesus again. I preferred not to sleep anyway but rather drink in the entire experience for what it was as the something strangely wonderful took shape. The women were singing hymns while a local pastor led everyone in prayers. The young men told jokes and listened to the radio while the old men played dominoes. A small group of my adult art students came by searching for me specifically to pray with, and then stayed to sing with everyone else.

Amidst it all I just lay on my back silently and watched the stars continue to fall, one by one, until it seemed only a few of the brightest ones remained in the sky.

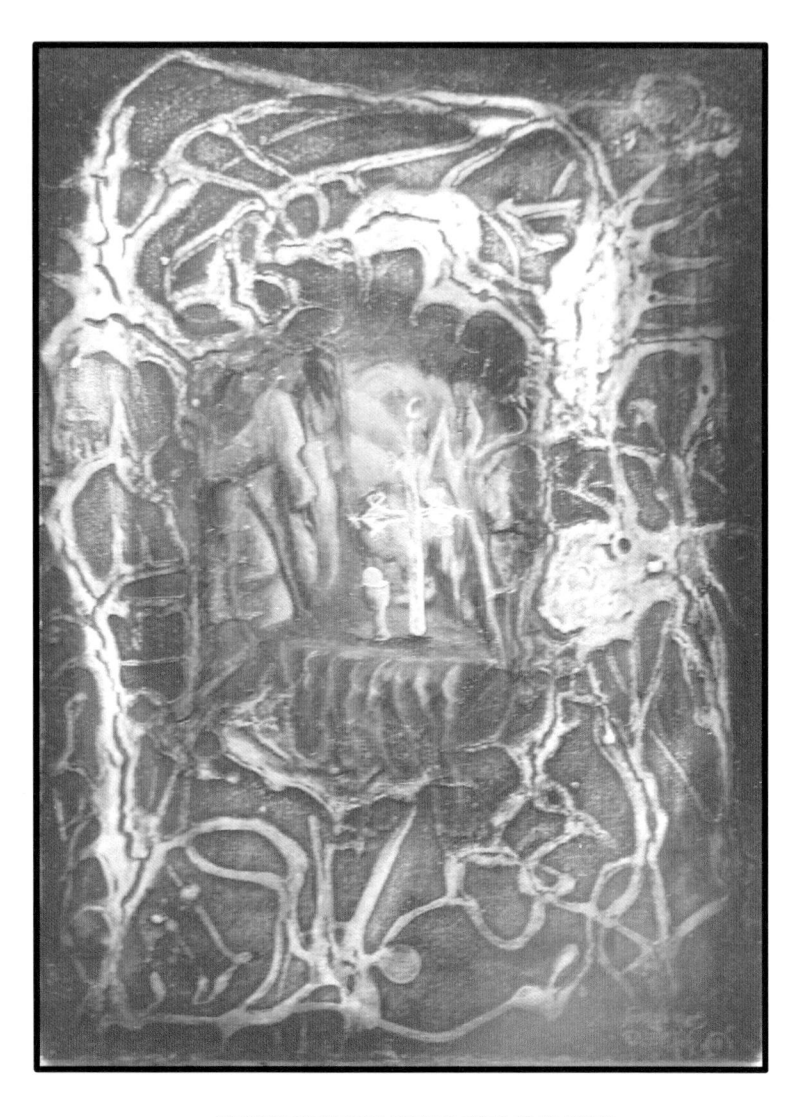

ARTWORK BY GEORGES DANIPY

REFUGEES OF FEAR

We all spent the night wondering if there would be another day for Haiti. About 12 hours after the original quake, the first rays of sunlight began to rise above the eastern mountains and shine upon the people of Mizak, bringing hope. This doesn't mean that it washed away all of the fears that had been stirred up, but at least for now, everyone knew that they were going to see at least one more day.

Berthony and I got up and went back to his house. As we walked Berthony finally began talking. Since the quake he had barely said a word and now, on the path to his house, he began to open up. I didn't even know yet where he was when it hit the day before and he didn't know for me either. We were both waiting to see if life would last long enough to make sharing worth it. So we shared our stories. For Berthony the fear that was shaken up inside of him that day went back a long time.

Ever since he was a small child, Berthony had always heard the old men in his community talk about the end of the world. "They had always warned us that it was coming soon, because the Bible says so." What he never heard them talk about was earthquakes. So naturally, when the ground started trembling, he assumed that he was witnessing what the old men always spoke about. This must be the End.

He was leaving school at the time, walking arm in arm with a cousin of his and they were talking about a neighbor who had been spreading rumors about their family. They were getting near to Berthony's house and were walking under the tall mango and coconut trees that rose out of his father's fields when their conversation was cut short by a monstrous rumbling noise coming from the north. Berthony didn't pay the noise much attention at first. Still being near the main road, he simply assumed that it was just one of the large, poorly maintained trucks that frequently passes by full of people and supplies coming from the city. But he soon realized that it was something more as he says, "The noise shook within our bodies before the ground ever shook beneath our feet." Then his cousin yelled "earthquake!" And let go of Berthony's arm to run away as fast as she could. But Berthony didn't even noticed what she said. He stood frozen as the earth beneath betrayed him. He heard the warnings of the old men echo through his head and was sure that the End had come. He looked up, disoriented, and felt like the trees around him were going to fall on top of him. His entire surroundings seemed to be imploding upon him. Unsure what to do, he crouched on the ground and covered his head with his hands and waited for the End to take him away.

A few seconds later the trembling stopped and he cautiously peered up through his fingers to see if the world he had closed his eyes to moments before was still there. When he looked at the trees above him he felt them still wavering ominously. So he sprang to his feet and ran to a nearby rocky hillside away from all trees and lay there flat on his back staring up at the sky hoping to find some answers. Remembering what he and his cousin had been discussing, he thought about all of the people who spend their time gossiping and spreading lies about their brothers and sisters and thought that that must have something to do with why this all was happening. He saw that there are too many people constantly tearing others down and unwilling to love and understand. In a world like that, God must have gotten tired of all the sin and decided to end it all for good. Lingering there, he thought about all of the mouths that he later said had broken my house.

Berthony still can't say exactly how long he lay there on his back on the rocks. It could have been a brief moment and it could have been hours. He can't remember the time that transpired there, but says it must not have been long because next thing he recalls he was back at his house where he found his cousin with his mother both screaming and crying.

When Julie noticed him she ran to him and threw her arms around him still wailing, unable to form words. "We thought you were dead," the cousin said. "When we went back to find you, we didn't see you where I left you. We thought a tree had fallen on you."

"I'm okay. I'm okay." He assured them, but in his own heart he still wasn't sure that any of them were safe. Still thinking this was just the beginning of the end, he feared the worst.

This fear gripped him in every fiber of his being. It rendered his tongue useless as he failed at converting thoughts into speech. It turned his stomach against him making him nauseous and unable to eat. It vibrated throughout his body making his legs unstable and his shoulders quiver. This fear only increased throughout the night as the aftershocks continued to wear away at his strength of mind and body.

Later that afternoon, after finding each other in front of the house, Berthony and I wandered the community together as two bodies with stagnant souls inside. When we arrived on the hilltop by my house searching for a place to sleep with the other neighbors Berthony recalled being offended that some of the other young men were actually telling jokes at a time like that. He was in no mood for jokes as he wrapped himself in the sheets from home and tried in vain to make himself believe that life would go on.

It wasn't until later, when I got in touch with my mother on the telephone that Berthony's outlook began to change. When I had gotten off the phone he asked me if the quakes were happening in my country too. When I told him that they had not passed by any other countries, Berthony says that that was the moment that he began to realize that it was not the end of the world, but a disaster that had only struck his country. And that realization helped Berthony to begin to find stillness. "It was like I had woken up from a trance," Berthony recalls. Although, even as we spoke in the path the day after, it was clear that the fear still hadn't abated, but he wasn't petrified of Armageddon either. It was still there reminding him how fragile life was as the aftershocks would come and go, but he was now able to move forward through the fear knowing that it was not the end of the world. It was not the end of life.

I held my brother's hand, both of us needing the extra strength of an empathetic friend as we walked on and shared. We passed by my skeleton of a home without offering it a second glance and went right on by to arrive at Berthony's. When we arrived, Julie gave us two chairs and brought us each a cup of the fresh coffee she had just brewed. Julie's thin little eyes were sad, but she was trying to be strong and keep taking care of her family. Sony and Joslyn were there with their father, Bebe, all recounting their experiences as well. I too shared mine and the family grieved for the house with me. People would come and go and tell "what they lived" in the earthquake with their families and friends and neighbors.

This is how they asked the question, "What did you live in the earthquake?" The focus was on life, because if we were there to tell our story we were alive. No one could ask what one experienced, or saw, or went through, because many experienced and saw and went through the earthquake, but not everyone lived. Anyone who was there to speak of it, must tell what they lived. And everyone wanted to hear everyone else's story because even though 9 million people experienced the same catastrophe at exactly the same time, no two people experienced it in the same way. Each individual in the country lived something different that day. So on the day after and in the days and weeks to come, that's all that we did was share our stories with one another. There was nothing else to talk about, nothing else that seemed to matter. This earthquake had suddenly redefined each of our lives from the moment that it started to quiver. For a while we could think of nothing else and we talked about nothing else. The stories were shared one after another being stitched together as the communal experience emerged to prove strength. For now it was under the shelter of those stories that we would hide. Each story was told adding its own dimension to the bigger picture of what this disaster was and what it meant for this tiny country as a whole.

After having sat there at the Gere's house for a couple hours, having regrouped personally in my mind, and as a family, I decided to move on. I didn't know where, but I needed to move. Sony too was becoming a little stir-crazy and suggested that we take a walk to look at some of the other homes that were seriously damaged in the area. I wasn't sure if I wanted to see the others. I was being selfish and felt that at that time that having seen my own was enough and perhaps I'd rather just sit and wallow in self-pity for a while longer before going to see what other families were suffering. Besides that, I was also acutely aware of what the scene of a white man walking around taking note of earthquake damage looks like. People begin hoping for rebuilding, reconstruction, and relief. People begin hoping for aid to come their way. I'd known that routine all too well having participated in damage assessment for disaster relief after hurricanes in the country in previous years. I'd been by their side through other struggles in this community and people had learned that they could depend on me and I knew that I would want to help my neighbors if I saw them without other hope.

But now it was different. Now everyone in the community knew that I needed relief in the same way that they all did. We were all in the same boat and that boat had capsized. Yet, somehow, I knew that I would still be seen as the only one who knew how to swim.

Nonetheless, I decided to go walking with Sony. Despite the awareness that I could do nothing with my heart's aching to change what I would see, I knew that absence in others' pain would not change anything either. I knew that people were hurting who sold me my weekly freezy pop in the market, or who had children that had splatter painted with me at a kid's club, or who had ridden on a motorcycle taxi with me to the city. I wanted to be present for them whether I could do anything for them or not.

We first passed by our neighbor's home whose family lost two houses. The larger one with four rooms was simply opened up like a dollhouse with all of the four outside walls and the roof collapsed but the intersecting interior walls still standing. The smaller house where some of the wife's family lived was simply crumpled like a deflated accordion. Then we went on to the house of an artisan whom I knew well, and she and her family were sitting on chairs on top of a pile of rubble that used to be their home. It was as if they didn't even notice that their home was destroyed, they were just sitting there on their chairs as they might every morning. They were perhaps so shocked that they didn't know what to do. I didn't know what to do either. We were all unsure of our current circumstances and maybe for that moment it seemed easier to pretend like yesterday didn't happen. The sadness in front of us was undeniable yet it was not appropriate to be sad just in case there was a chance that we would still wake up from this nightmare and see things the way they were on January 11th.

Sony and I kept walking. We passed by many other homes in the neighborhood, some with large chunks of wall having fallen, others with large cracks in the cement, and some seemingly untouched.

It was a phenomenon that was truly impossible to wrap one's mind around why the spectrum of damage ranged so vastly amongst houses so near to each other. For example, Julie and Bebe's house saw only some exterior stucco flake off during the trembling, while my home just up the hill about 200 meters was laid to ruin, yet the HAPI health clinic which is right in between the two, was in absolutely perfect shape. At the same time, my next-door neighbor, had two small houses side by side; one was undamaged while the other was pulverized to a pile of dust. This trend, or lack of a trend, ran true throughout the community. There was no explaining why one house would topple while the next stood firm.

It all was enough to make one really question his entire understanding of the cosmos and his place in it. For me, in the beginning, every tragic truth that I witnessed was one more reason adding to my doubt and my anger towards God. I'll admit that even before the quake I never really knew what to believe after all of the suffering that I'd seen existing in perfect harmony with all of the beauty on the earth. But along with all the cement walls in that country, whatever beliefs I had were shaken right to the ground with the quake as confusion and bitterness began to sink in. I also learned early on, however, that I was quite alone in this sense because the Haitians around me were finding more reasons fortifying their beliefs. They had very clear explanations of God's role in it all and these explanations became integral parts of their personal stories.

Jesus and Satan had gotten together one day to chat and after a while they started to argue. They were arguing over which one of them had more followers in Haiti. Satan was telling Jesus that obviously he had the most followers in this country because everyone knew they were all really a bunch of voodoo practitioners and all that stuff on Sundays was just for show. Jesus was telling Satan, "You know that's not true. They're constantly praying to me and you know that when they all really need someone to talk to they come to me first. All that voodoo stuff's just for fun, they don't really believe it." And so the two of them were going back and forth like this for a long time, "I have more followers," "No, I have more followers," "They all love me more," "No, they all love me more," And finally Jesus said, "Okay, fine Satan, if you need me to prove it to you, I'll prove it to you." They had reached this point in the argument at 4:53, on Tuesday, January 12th. That's the point that Jesus unleashed the 7.0 earthquake upon Haiti. Ten seconds later he stilled the earth and told Satan, "Listen… you hear that?" It was the sound of every Haitian in the country crying out the name of Jesus. "See, I told ya." He said.

Along our walk, we ran into my good friend, Jona Douge, who shared with us his newly intensified devotion. The day before, he was one of those more than 9 million Haitians crying out Jesus' name. But it was not unusual for Jona to cry that name. He had always considered himself a faithful Christian and had even talked about becoming a pastor, but January 12th gave his praise a whole new perspective. He had just survived something that hundreds of thousands of his Haitian brothers and sisters did not survive. And so he praised. For life, for breath, for grace, he praised.

Earlier in the day, all that he had to be thankful for were the mandarins that were plentiful on the trees in his area that time of year. That's what he was doing when Jesus and Satan started arguing, he was harvesting mandarins. His nephew, was up in the tree picking the fruit and Jona was on the ground catching them. Jona had stopped for a moment to peel one of the mandarins to eat when all of a sudden he looked around and saw all of the trees around him quivering. Then he felt the earth rise up under his feet and tried to run but he took two steps and stumbled to fall on the ground. From the ground where he was he cried out, "It's the end of the world!" Then he remembered his nephew still up in the tree. "Get down from there! The world is ending!" But the nephew was too scared to even move and stayed perched in the branches where he was. Jona stayed right where he was too until the earth stopped quaking. Then he got up on his feet and motioned up into the tree, "It's okay, you can come down now. The trembling has passed." But he still wouldn't move. He stayed fixed where he was clinging to the branches. Jona went and got a ladder and retrieved his nephew himself.

When they were both safe on the ground, they ran together to search for Jona's other nieces and nephews at the house. They found two hiding under the bed, one crouched in the corner of the kitchen, and the rest holding each other's hands in the field. But Jona was still very worried because they didn't see his father. He walked to all of his neighbors' houses to see if he could find him, but he says the whole time that he walked from house to house he wasn't even aware of what he was doing. He was a zombie void of emotion or conscience. Not seeing his father anywhere, he ended up returning to the same tree where he had been picking mandarins. He lay down under the tree, closed his eyes, and reflected on what was happening.

Matthew 24 came to his mind, where the disciples ask Jesus what the signs of the end of the age will be, "Nation will rise against nation and kingdom against kingdom. There will be famines and earthquakes in various places. All these are the beginning of birth pains."

"Is this supposed to be a test of our faith?" Jona wondered. He had never known anything as terrible as this in his life and he was questioning how he was supposed to make it through this trial.

Jona felt someone touch his shoulder and he opened his eyes to see his father knelt down next to him. "Come inside, Jona," his father said, "we're all here. Come in." But Jona refused. He had decided that if this was the end of the world, he was going to die right there under that tree. He let his father leave him and go back to the house while he stayed on the ground, closed his eyes once again, and surrendered himself to whatever fate would befall him there.

He says that he can't say that the thoughts that were passing through his head at that point were really prayers, but they were definitely fixed on his Creator because Jona felt that he would soon be meeting Bondye face to face.

Soon he heard singing in the distance. He heard praises being sung to God. He was afraid to open his eyes thinking that he might find that he had arrived in Heaven before the choruses of angels. When he decided to be brave and slowly peek, all that he saw was the mandarin tree still above him. So he got up and listened closer to see if he could tell where the singing was coming from. He yelled to his nephew again to tell him to come with him in search of the music. He didn't know what was going to happen and decided that if he was going to die, he didn't want to die alone.

As the two of them walked they heard the music get closer and closer until they came upon a gathering of their neighbors praying under a large tent. They allowed themselves to be absorbed into the congregation of others who were waiting for the world to end. "And we just started singing," Jona says. And they sang until 5:00 the next morning. All through the night their songs seemed to be tuned to the metronome of aftershocks that passed by frequently. You could almost count on the ground shifting after every fourth song. Every time another tremor came everyone stopped singing and just cried Jesus' name. Then they'd wait for the stillness to return before someone would start up the song right where they left off. No one slept that night, only praised.

"We all really believed that Jesus might be returning any minute. That was the only explanation that made any sense to us. We've never been taught about earthquakes besides what it mentions in the Bible. So, the only logical response was to praise," Jona recalls.

They didn't question God. They didn't even ask for help. They weren't angry with God or doubtful of his presence. They were simply overwhelmed with such a profound sense of reverence for his undeniable power and might in those moments that they could not resist the impulse to release the worship that was erupting from the deepest corridors of their souls.

"The chance to worship together is the only thing that kept many of us sane following the quake," Jona said. He had become very depressed as he failed to wrap his mortal mind around this phenomenon. So he kept returning to the only thing that made sense, praise. Tremors continued to shake the ground beneath their feet but nothing could shake their faith.

"How could you praise a god that just decided to kill so many of your friends and neighbors?" I pressured. "How can you even believe that a god truly exists in the midst of so much ugliness and pain?"

I thought that I would get some reaction out of Jona, maybe a small suggestion of doubt underneath his early emotional worship. Having participated in a Bible study with Jona before and having had many philosophical conversations with him while sitting on ancient graves out in front of the guest house where I lived, I had gotten to know Jona as a very critical and analytical believer who was always willing to question what he read or what others told him about God. But on that day after the quake hearing his story in the road, there were no questions to be asked, just simple praise. For life, for breath, for grace, he continued to praise.

Jona wasn't the only one whose initial response was turning to God. As Sony and I walked through the streets that day we heard others share their stories of spiritual encounters during the quake. One woman we talked to was returning from the market in a nearby community and was carrying a large basket of merchandise on her head when the quake struck. "When the earth started quaking," she told us, "I dropped the load that was on my head and fell to my knees to pray. The ground was still again before my knees even hit it."

Yvette Jean-Jacques, a young woman whom I worked with, told us that even though she had always believed in God, the earthquake of the day before had proved his power far beyond anything she ever knew. "If I had just a single drop of belief in God before," she said, "I now have an ocean."

* * *

Shortly after I started daydreaming at the clinic, I sat with Jona and Yvette in a small alleyway between two walls behind the community center to timidly and carefully explore the next crazy idea together. Two others joined us, Serge Gabriel and Kesnel Tondreau, to ask the forbidden question, "Was a new organization even needed in this area and could we, a bunch of kids in the eyes of nonprofit professionals, actually pull it off?"

If anyone could do it, it was these four. I had known most of them since the beginning and had learned from them what extreme potential lay unacknowledged in the dreams of the young adults here who were wanting to make a difference. I had witnessed them being taken advantage of by other organizations that didn't understand how to activate that potential. In their hands I could imagine just how the communal beauty that naturally exists here could grow to change the way people live. And that is exactly the kind of art project that I wanted to be involved in, one where human lives became the media with which to create something extraordinary.

This is where it would start, but it would take a lot of work on the part of us all. These four were all right around my age and still struggling to make it out of high school. I knew that if any of them had been born in a different place with the opportunities that my birthplace afforded me, then they would each already have at least one college degree under their belts and be working as successful young professionals and making good money in whatever fields they chose. They were smart, talented, and stuck in a system that smothers dreams. They were the gifted ones who had the drive to really initiate significant change within their society but they would never get the chance in the current system.

Most organizations choose to focus on different demographics that conjure up pity from potential donors. It's not as attractive to donors to have photos of healthy, clean, well-dressed young adults on your website as it is to have hungry, neglected children, or marginalized women, or victims of war or violence. Most organizations choose to focus on the negative and view a society's problems as needing to be fixed. Those of us who sat there that day agreed that it was time for an organization that concentrated its vision on what was beautiful and good about a society and work to grow that beauty to overcome the ugliness. We began discussing specific programs that could fulfill such a vision and together, the five of us founded Living Media International.

After that we decided not to waste any time. I had agreed to work with HAPI until the end of January 2010, so we set the official first day for Living Media as February 1.

* * *

In hearing people's perceptions of God after the quake, I was surprised to notice that even such devoted conviction did not necessarily translate to courage. For Jona, he was still terrified of what he felt. Even as we stood there and talked in the street he said that he felt like he was trembling. At that moment he said that he couldn't believe that that feeling of quaking would ever go away.

The earthquake had thrown off everyone's equilibrium both physically and mentally. As the aftershocks continued it was impossible to know whether the sensation we consistently felt was just our heart beating within our chest or the ground trembling beneath our feet. A tremor could come through and we would have to look around to see if everyone else felt it also to know if it was real or if our knees were still just weak and wobbly form the original quake. It seemed as if Mother Nature was just playing games with us and it scared me to imagine what the results of such mind games would have in the following days when an entire population was effected. I was beginning to feel the strands of my surety unravel and I knew others felt it too. I saw it in their eyes as we walked by in the road.

Complicating the whole situation and compounding people's mental and physical instability was the fact that cell phone communication was still impossible throughout the day. When Sony and I arrived back at his family's home, everyone was sitting there speculating on the fate of their loved ones in Port-au-Prince and other areas. Without being able to call them no one knew whether the ones they loved most were dead or alive or injured or homeless or what. Julie and Bebe now had five children in Port-au-Prince at the time of the quake, and over 24 hours after it struck they had no idea if any of them were okay. All that they knew was what they heard in the news which told them that the city was in dust and early death toll estimates in the hundreds of thousands, some even millions, were being reported. Some rumors were starting to spread by word of mouth, but until you spoke to your loved ones directly, you couldn't be sure what to believe because information gets mixed up so easily. Everyone was extremely worried for those that they had in the city, but there was nothing that they could do at that point except wait and pray.

Throughout the day we shared our stories and we waited to hear others. We prayed for those that we had not heard from yet and hoped that their stories were of "what they lived".

That evening we had to decide where to sleep again, joining the rest of the refugees in the community seeking a safe place to lie down for the night. Some refugees try to escape war, discrimination, famine, or even natural disaster, but it was clear that night that even though it was an earthquake that caused Haitians to leave their homes initially, at that point, it was pure fear that kept them from returning. It was fear that kept them laying in the streets and out on the hillsides. No one was trying to cross any borders or hide from imminent danger, they had just moved into their backyards. But if you saw the way they were all living you'd still swear that they were in a refugee camp. Little clusters of makeshift tents and people sleeping on the ground. Yes, the post-earthquake people of Haiti were a different breed of refugee. They were so afraid to sleep in their houses that finding the perfect rock to sleep on had almost become a game and seeing who could build the most elaborate shelter out of sheets and leaves, a community wide contest.

Berthony and I took our sheets and blankets under our arms and entered the game heading off to the rocky hill where he had laid the day before after running away from the trees that he feared falling on him. We found about 20 people there already having staked out their places to sleep for the night. Some were leaning palm branches on each other to create teepee like shelters, while others started stringing bed sheets and tarps between tree branches. Still others just laid their blankets on the rocks and their unsteady bodies on the blankets. Papi was there with one of his brothers and we found a relatively flat spot next to them and staked out our own bed and lay down. Soon after lying down, a neighborhood voodoo priestess, came by with a rosary given to her by some American mission team the previous summer and prayed with some individuals in the camp. That night my whole perspective on refugees was transformed as I became one myself. I wasn't one of the refugees one might find on the Help Refugees website, but I, and all my friends and neighbors, were trying to escape something nonetheless.

Ever since I had arrived in Mizak I had thought that it would have been enjoyable to sleep outside. The weather is so nice and the stars so beautiful, I had always thought that sleeping outdoors would have been beyond serene, but if I ever mentioned it to my friends they thought I was crazy because if you sleep outside you'll undoubtedly be eaten by a dyab, a monster. Until the earthquake, anyway, they would have never entertained such a foolish idea as camping outdoors because they were afraid of the creatures that may lurk in the dark of night. But on this night, they had forgotten about all that and laid down in the most open areas they could find. I guess at that point they were more afraid of being crushed by falling cement than being devoured by a demon. So we all took our chances, and built our local refugee camps, and prayed a lot. We had survived one more day and began believing that life would go on.

ARTWORK BY ALEXANDRA AMAZAN

TAKING STEPS

Soon after awaking the next day we found that some people had started to find telephone communication to other parts of the country, but still very few at first. This allowed more rumors to begin trickling in about our loved ones in other regions, so we tried to confirm which ones were true. We spent our time that day waiting to hear whom we'd lost and whom we would be able to see once more. I began receiving very positive rumors about my close friends but unsure of the sources still, it was impossible to believe anything 100%. Yet we were hearing more and more names of people who had left Mizak for work or for school in the city and would never return. There were only a handful of deaths that actually occurred in the Mizak area but everyone there was soon finding out that they had lost other family members in Jacmel or in Port-au-Prince.

Many of these rumors were being spread by scattered cell phone connections but others were also starting to arrive through firsthand accounts from survivors returning from the city. As soon as the quake hit two days earlier many people from the cities first response was to escape and they did that however they found possible. With the roads impassable from rockslides and crevices in the middle of the asphalt, some resolved to just escape the horror by foot.

That morning we sat there in front of Julie's house waiting to hear of the condition of the family. People would come and go sharing news that they had heard, but it was when Rodrigue Badio showed up in the courtyard that everyone rubbed their eyes to see if it was truly him. Rodrigue was a neighbor who had been in Port-au-Prince for school and no one expected to see him that day. It was about 1:00 in the afternoon when he showed up after having walked all the way from the city. It was through him that we really got our first glimpse of the absolute terror that had descended on the capitol. Ever since the ground began trembling, Rodrigue had been walking. He took us back to those first steps that he remembered.

Step. Step. Step. Rodrigue was walking. He was walking through a street past people who couldn't walk. They were missing legs or feet or were caught under rubble. Both of his feet were beneath him and they were walking. Like a phantom of himself, he pressed on through the streets. He couldn't tell you where he just came from and definitely had no destination in mind. When you're walking through hell you don't care where you end up or how you got there, you just move. So he walked placing one foot in front of the other and with each step that he took, fear grew.

All he remembered was sitting in his school in Kafou, taking notes, when he heard what he thought was the generator starting up. Then all the kids around him jumped up and ran, clogging the door as the walls began to crack and fall.

Next thing he knew, there he was, in the street, quite a distance away from his school. He had no idea how he got there. *Step. Step.* He had been in some sort of daze, completely unaware of his surroundings, until a frantic man bumped into him with a wheelbarrow and shouted, "Hey kid, watch it! You can't just stand there! Something will fall on your head and crush you!" So he took a step to the side out of his way and looked into his wheelbarrow as the man hurried by him. Lying inside in a mangled mess were two bodies soaked in blood, limbs dangling over the edge like overcooked spaghetti. Rodrigue didn't know why this man was carrying around dead corpses. Then one of the bloody spaghetti arms reached out and touched his leg. He looked into the pile of injured anatomy and connected a terrified gaze with two eyes peering out of a swollen skull and matted filthy hair. A woman, not much older than him, seemed to tell him with those eyes, "Tell tomorrow hello for me, because I shall not see it."

"Get going man! Seriously!" The wheelbarrow pusher shouted again. Rodrigue started moving, now quicker. *Step, step, step, step.* He started walking through the street. As he did he began looking around and found himself completely incapable of comprehending anything that he saw. All that he saw was death, but he kept taking steps towards an unknown future. He thought to himself that he was going to disappoint that girl in the wheelbarrow because it was starting to seem that none of them would be around to greet tomorrow. He thought that he had seen his last tomorrow.

His feet moved forward beneath him as his ears fixed on sounds unlike any he had ever heard. There were screams all around from people running by, from under piles of cement, from inside wheelbarrows. People were saying to run to higher ground because there were going to be tidal waves coming. Others were saying it was no use running because they all were going to die regardless. People were saying this was the End. It was as if he was walking through some sort of nightmare that he happened upon by accident. He felt as if he was walking upstream but was sure that no one knew where they were actually going so he kept moving.

He moved past sights that he had never seen before and could have never imagined. He saw hundreds of people wandering covered in dust and debris and blood as if they had just crawled out of graves from death itself. Some touched him as they walked by and he feared they might take him with them back to the death that they came from. He walked by a gas station that had collapsed and exploded into flames incinerating everything in its vicinity. There were cars and motorcycles charred black with the bodies of their drivers and passengers scorched lying inside or on the ground next to them. He saw one building completely opened up and inside kneeling on the floor in front of a computer still glowing was the body of man decapitated by the falling rubble. Rodrigue saw children, so many children lost and scared and mixed up in a world that was impossible for them to understand. Rodrigue felt the same way, lost and scared. But he kept walking. With everything he saw and everything he heard, the fear continued to grow. *Step. Step. Step.*

He walked all through the night until he found himself outside of the city limits. He walked until the toppled houses became less dense and began walking through some fields. *Step. Step...* Stop. He stood and listened to the night around him. He heard the nighttime breeze travel through the fields and rustle the dry leaves of the corn stalks. He closed his eyes and recognized that he was alive. He heard crickets chirp and a dog barking somewhere in the distance. It was a stark change from the sounds that he had heard in the city. There was no screaming or crying now. He listened closer beyond the noise of the dog and he heard people's voices. Was it singing or more collective wailing? He couldn't be sure of anything but the voices sounded peaceful and the melody lured him toward them. He took another step and headed in their direction.

He entered a small rural community where he found something that he had not seen yet, groups of people lying together outside. It was in these groups that people were lifting up their voices in prayer and song. Among these people he stopped for more than a moment for the first time since he found himself outside of his school, interrupting the rhythm of his constant steps. When he did stop he realized how tired he was and he laid down there with these strangers where he felt his fear could rest. He had no idea what time it was, but laid there until daybreak, unable to sleep, but at least he was still.

As the sun came up, he rose to his feet again and continued walking. After the few hours of stillness his mind had stilled too and his body was no longer on autopilot. He asked directions to get back to the main road that he knew would lead him to Mizak and he continued to walk. Once on the road he began asking for motorcycles to take him the rest of the way but none were circulating. He heard of the damage to the road all along the way and decided that the only way for him to get back there would be to keep walking.

All through the day he walked, now on a path that he was familiar with, but had never taken by foot before. Usually he would take a bus from Kafou to Mizak, which would take about two hours, but with no other options, his feet tasted this pavement for the first time and he headed in the direction of home. It was during this time that he first became aware of what he had left behind. He carried nothing with him, only the dusty clothes on his back. For the last two years he had been attending school in the city and all of his possessions were there, but the day before he began walking straight from the school and hadn't looked back. He didn't even know the condition of the house that he was living in or whether his older brother that lived with him was okay. But at that point along the road he had nothing to do but move forward. Hell was behind him and the only direction he wanted to go was away from it.

He walked all that day and into the night again when he found another community of people to spend the night with. These strangers, like the ones the night before, did not know Rodrigue and he did not know them. He had no idea what any of them experienced the day before, who or what they had lost. He had no idea how many of them were wanderers like himself, in transit, trying to arrive somewhere that felt right. Yet that night, he knew he was in the presence of others who didn't need to know him. At that point they were all one.

The next morning he continued his journey and after a couple hours reached Decouze. This was the last community on the road before reaching Jacmel and heading up into the mountains of LaVallee where Mizak is located. Here Rodrigue started to notice some motorcycles in the street. He flagged one down and asked if the road was clear from there to LaVallee and the chauffeur confirmed that it was. The driver said "I'll take you there for $400 Haitian dollars". That trip would usually cost no more than 30 but the driver explained how absurdly high gas prices had shot up since the quake and how so few drivers were even on the road.

Rodrigue felt like he couldn't walk anymore. He dug in his pocket and pulled out $250 Haitian dollars. The driver looked at it and told him to hop on.

When Rodrigue finally arrived in front of Julie's house that afternoon he was visibly exhausted and each of us sitting there felt completely overwhelmed having heard his story. Each of us there wanted to ask him more details especially about the area of the city where Julie and Bebe's other children lived, in Martissant, but we couldn't pressure him at that point. He'd been through enough and wasn't even home yet. We'd continue to rest on rumors for now. Julie touched his shoulder and told him to quit wasting his time with us. His mother needed to see him.

Rodrigue took a deep breath with the realization that he had almost arrived. He stood up and took another step, now with an energy that defied his physical fatigue. *Step, step, step, step.* He walked around the corner of Julie's house and down the path through the field of congo beans towards his family's home.

After having sat and listened to Rodrigue's story I felt like I needed to get up and walk somewhere as well. Just sitting all day and listening to the news of who had died was exhausting in itself. So I walked up the hill to my house deciding that I was ready to face it again. I found Papi there sitting on the ground out front with his back to the house, seeming to ponder the unbelievable reality of what was behind him. I approached him and he raised his head slowly to look me in the eyes but said nothing. I kept silent as well. We didn't need to say anything. A long sigh and slow blink from me and a shake of his head with a Haitian tongue click from him communicated everything. We stood there for a moment looking at each other silently saying everything that we knew about the house through our eyes. Then I bent down, picked up a softball-sized rock, and hurled it at the side of what was left of the house knocking off another small chunk of cement. Papi started laughing and let out a prolonged, "Heeeeeeyyyy," letting me know that he approved of the idea. The house was destroyed and we were going to have to tear it completely down again before starting over anyway and we were angry at the world so we might as well throw rocks. I picked up two more and threw them as Papi watched with a smile.

I plopped down next to Papi on the ground and nudged him with my shoulder as we began talking in our usual fashion, with as few words as possible. Papi had a succinct ability to make himself understood and to understand others without all the extra words that most people would choose to use. As we talked, we first shared the updates that we had gathered throughout the morning of all the people that we knew in the cities. We had received basically the same information so far and were still waiting to hear more details on some stories.

While we were sitting there Marjorie came walking up the hillside on her way to Julie's house. It was the first time that we had seen her since the quake. As soon as the earthquake passed on Tuesday, she immediately searched for a motorcycle to take her down to Jacmel. All of her two brothers and four sisters lived down there and she had rushed to see how they were. Now she returned and although we had already heard the news by telephone of the family, I wanted to hear the details from her directly. I took her hand and asked her about her sister, Isabel, as she sat down next to us. With tears in her eyes she told us what happened.

Isabel was in a small alleyway between her house and her neighbor's washing clothes with her two-year-old son, John Kerby, playing in the next room with two neighbor children. Her older 6-year-old son was at his aunt's house after school. As she did the laundry Isabel heard a rumbling noise, "Kip. Kip. Kip." Then everything went black. The house was shaking and walls collapsing. She looked at the foundation of the three-story building that she lived in and it seemed to be melting. The neighbor's house tipped towards her and she jumped up and grabbed on to an iron door behind her. As she grabbed a hold the door split off from the cement wall it was attached to and fell to the ground taking Isabel back down with it. "Jesus save me!" She cried.

The entire building had tipped over at an angle and the earth was still shaking. She scaled the fallen wall in front of her to reach a window where she thought she could get into the room where her baby was playing. She reached the window and looked in to see the children still sitting on the floor. At the very moment that she looked at them, before she was able to climb through and grab them, she watched as the entire wall on the opposite side fell forwards on top of all three toddlers bringing the entire three story building toppling down with it.

In the alleyway where Isabel was the fallen structure had created a triangular tunnel through which she was able to easily walk out and into the street. There in the street she looked back at the building. She saw the top story collapsed on top of a disintegrated pile of rubble of the first two stories and knew that her baby was underneath it all. All around her was chaos. Light poles were popping and electric lines snapping as dust filled the air and peoples' screams came from all directions. Isabel added her screams to the agonized song of the moment and cried for her child that could not be saved.

Two days later as Marjorie sat there and talked to Papi and I they still were unable to make any effort to finding the body of John Kerby. Marjorie described the situation in Jacmel to us and how many homes had collapsed and how many people were waiting for help to remove rubble from off of their loved ones but nothing was being done yet. Even at that moment, Marjorie said she couldn't stay long. She had just hurried up the mountain to see Julie's family and give them the details on the family in Jacmel, and then she was going to go right back to be with her sister at this time.

No one could blame her. At that time the most important thing that any of us felt we could do was be present with the ones we loved. I was fortunate to have my Haitian family present for us all to support one another, but I was also reaching out to my loved ones back in the states for support as well. Thanks to communications opening up with Digicel I was able to talk to my mother and my brother that day to follow up on the static filled message that my mother received two nights earlier. Reconnecting with my family and my native culture began changing the way I perceived my own situation. Since the moment of the quake we had all just been trying to survive each moment and hadn't been thinking too far beyond where our next step would land. Americans like to plan for the future, though, which is something I hadn't spent any of my energy on since the quake.

I had been working towards embarking on a new beginning as of February 1st, but fate would have it that I, along with all Haitians, would be finding a new beginning on January 13th instead. At that point it was still too early to really know quite how we would move forward with our plans for LMI. The goal was to start an organization that didn't portray its members or beneficiaries as victims. Now the earthquake had struck and made us all victims in one way or another, and that was going to change everything. As soon as that label, "victim" is attached to someone, dignity becomes harder to recapture. Yet while everyone was concentrated on just finding out whether their families were alive, it seemed irrelevant to think about all that.

The culture that had birthed me was expecting immediate plans for action. But the culture that had adopted me was only concerned if all of its children were alright. In my position bridging the two I was possibly too close to the situation to effectively respond to an emergency such as some would expect. I had just reconnected with the place that could get me resources and aid if needed, but I was still feeling pretty helpless. My mind and my spirit were not ready to coordinate any relief because I was busy sleeping with the community on the rocks and singing hymns with them and keeping them company while they waited for news. I needed to be present with them in the moment and let them know that I would be there for them through this tragedy rather than running off to search for momentary relief. I knew how quickly the TV cameras and relief teams would lose interest and fade from the scene but the something strangely wonderful that knit that community together would still remain. That's what I wanted to be a part of.

In situations such as this people start looking for heroes. And as a white man in that situation, an inverted racism expected me to be one. The Haitians there had been disappointed by plenty of foreigners pretending to be their heroes before and now understood that I was there for different reasons. It was the people who look like me who like to draw their human-separating lines that imagined people like me in the trenches throwing rubble off of bodies and caring for people's broken bones and severed limbs. They were waiting to hear stories of people sheltered who were left homeless and babies cared for who had lost their parents and were left crying in the streets. They were expecting to hear stories of how lives were being saved. A photo in the news of a sweaty white guy in a bandana carrying a crying baby out from the devastation of collapsed buildings somehow signifies hope while the story of Isabel Gere goes unnoticed becoming just one more in the masses of those who mourn.

This dissidence between my cultural influences wore away at my own courage as time went on. There were some dark corners in my spirit that I had refused to acknowledge at first but light began to shine on them as the environment in Haiti changed. I had trouble keeping up with the evolution of it all, from the original natural disaster, to a news story, to a humanitarian crisis; it was still my home and I was trying to survive in it right along with the others around me.

There wasn't much I could do. At least I could throw rocks at my house to let the earthquake know that I wasn't going to let it beat me without putting up a fight.

ARTWORK BY JOHNNY GABRIEL

JACMEL

After having talked to Majorie, the next morning I decided that I needed to see things in the city for myself. In just the previous two days I had heard so many people talk about what the damage was like in Jacmel but I also knew what storytellers Haitians are and how that can lead to exaggerations. People had been saying that the city had been completely flattened and there was nothing left. I couldn't sit up there in Mizak anymore, so close to it all and not witness it with my own eyes so I went to take a look. Berthony and I found a motorcycle taxi and took the half hour ride down into the city.

As we entered the city with the Goosline River on our right and the houses of Jacmel emerging on our left, we began seeing some buildings collapsed as we passed by. Zooming by on a motorcycle, however, noticing rubble tucked back away from the road didn't feel real yet. Once we got into the edge of the city we got off the bike at the National gas station to take the rest of the way by foot. But Berthony and I really didn't know where to go. We had heard the names of some of the most damaged places, but at that point neither of us were experts on Jacmel geography so we just started wandering through the city. We would ask directions to some places while meandering but this took us on a very indirect route. As we walked through the center of town, down the main road, Route Barbaquilla, and up to the central plaza, we saw some moderate damage, but it was definitely not the Jacmel that I had been hearing about that was pulverized to a pile of dust. I was confused but we kept walking.

As we went down from the plaza, the first really serious damage that we encountered was the police station and prison. It was, in fact, the only location we saw all day that was taped off and prohibited for the public to approach. I had heard it said that all of the prisoners were either killed in the collapse or escaped. In the last few days they had started to find some of those criminals who escaped, but there were no prisons left to send them back to so the police would just shoot them on the spot and add them to the piles of bodies to be disposed of. They didn't even need any proof or trial. Someone just had to yell, "Stop, thief!" and Bam! Another corpse to add to the masses.

Moving on from the police station down towards Lakou New York beach, we began seeing more buildings flattened on the ground. Houses, schools, stores. Some I only knew because I remembered them from before, but passing by them then they were unrecognizable. Remnants of walls and piles of rubble remained of what used to be businesses and institutions of the city. We passed by Chery's

CyberCafe where I had gone to work on the internet just the day before the quake. It was located on the first floor of a two-story building which had now become a one-story building as the top floor crushed the bottom where I used to sit and catch up on emails. This chilling realization that I would have been a statistic had the earthquake hit 24 hours sooner made each subsequent step through life seem more fragile.

We went through the artisan district and saw a few of the popular shops ruined with papier-mâché masks and canvas paintings laying destroyed under the rubble. This is where we ran into a few people that we knew and they helped us find the school of St. Trinity, which we had heard was one of the worst. We could tell that we were getting close when we started seeing people wearing dust masks in the street. Some people had told us to not even go there because the smell was so bad. But I felt like I had to see it to make it real in my mind. So as we got near we put on our surgical masks which I had brought from the clinic. We entered the front gate and I snapped a photo of the flattened concrete that used to be a three story building. Then a man nearby said, "If he wants to see the bodies he has to go down around the back way."

I wasn't sure if I did want to see the bodies. I had made it through 25 years of my life without ever seeing a dead body besides in a casket, and I had a feeling that life would be more comfortable if I left it that way. Yet, I knew that if I didn't look at them that wouldn't make them not be there. They were there, right around the corner, and I needed to see them in order to understand this event beyond crumbling cement. I left Berthony in the street. He was 22-years-old, and I guess he decided that he preferred to keep life comfortable for now.

When I went around back I snapped another quick photo of the building from that angle. It wasn't until I lowered the camera that I even noticed the bodies. It was difficult to even distinguish the random limbs and swollen body parts from the debris of the school. There was a leg here, an arm there, and then an entire torso extending out from the layers of cement. I had heard that they had already removed a lot from this site over the previous few days but it was clear that there were still dozens if not hundreds more left to be uncovered. However, no one was working on uncovering them at that moment. No one was there at all. I looked around and the place was completely abandoned. I was the only person even acknowledging that this tragedy in front of me existed. So I got a little closer.

I didn't get too close still because all of those bodies had been there for three days and the smell was so strong that my little clinic mask didn't do much good. I got just close enough that I didn't want to look down to know exactly what I was stepping on any more. I breathed shallowly but took my time to examine what was before me. The hard part was over, I had seen the bodies. Now I needed to understand them.

There was one body in particular of a young man that intrigued and disturbed me as I stared. I got close enough to him that if I had a short stick in my hand I could have reached out and touched him with it. The top half of his body was exposed, the cement crushing him at his waist. His right hand was gripping onto a bunch of rebar with his arm bent at the elbow and his head resting in the crook. His other hand was extended out in front of him and the hand was lying gently on the leg of another body that was completely under the cement. His face was unrecognizable from the cement and debris that covered it but I couldn't help but stand there, unable to do anything but look, and think about the human that he was. This young man had a story to be told, but it would never be heard.

I wondered if this young man's path had ever crossed with my own. He could have easily sold me a phone card before or stood in front of me at a local concert. He could have been a friend to one of the multiple students that I knew that attended classes at UNASMOH, the university that held classes there and had just opened up for the semester the day before the quake, January 11. I had heard some of their stories already and was now able to picture those that they had spoken of who were not as fortunate as they were to make it out alive.

Francois Jean-Jacques, Yvette's brother, was one of these fortunate students. He was in Applied Mathematics at the time. He usually sat on the third bench from the front, but for some reason on this day he decided to sit on the second bench instead. All of the students were talking about what they had done over Christmas break and wishing each other a happy New Year. No one was really interested in the math problems that the professor was explaining on the board. The professor had given the students some problems to solve but they were all joking around and making too much noise to even notice the sound approaching. *Goudougoudou* came the noise. But then the benches started to shake and Francois says that he heard the walls and ceiling rip apart. The teacher jumped up and cried, "Earthquake," then started to run.

A girl from the front row bolted up and jumped on his back screaming, "Save me!" The teacher ran with her to the window from the second story classroom where they were and threw her out onto the roof of the latrine below. Other students started running to him and he would take them and throw them out onto the toilet roof one by one.

Francois got up but didn't run to the window. He ran out into the hallway, with only his pen in his hand, but the stairway was packed with students trying to get down and out of the building. The students were fighting and hitting each other to try to make it through. As he looked down at the mass of terrified young people he saw a huge chunk of cement fall from above and land on a man splitting him in two. At that he decided that going down could only mean death, so he decided to go up.

He looked at the stairway headed upward and said that it was as if dark clouds had opened up before him to show him the path to survival. He went to the third floor where he exited onto a large balcony. Standing there he could feel the building disintegrating under his feet. He had to act fast. There were three other young men on the balcony with him that all panicked and jumped into trees but the branches broke as they each tried to grab a hold and they plummeted to the ground. Francoise watched as they each crashed onto the cement below. He heard bones break, but he didn't have time to calculate, he knew that jumping was his only chance too. He ran and hurled himself toward the trunk of the closest tree, colliding with it abruptly and grabbing a hold as tight as he could. He held on and allowed himself to slide down to where his feet could reach the outer wall of the school grounds. He got off of the tree and balanced himself on the wall.

He turned around and watched the entire building crumble down on top of his classmates, teachers, and friends. He looked over at the latrine and saw several people still standing on top of it along with his teacher who was now on the ground helping others down off of the roof. Others were running from the building covered in debris. Still more could be heard screaming from inside as the whole school building crushed them.

Francois turned and jumped down on the other side of the wall that he was standing on. Once on solid ground, Francois just ran. Taking steps faster than he ever had before unsure whether Death was chasing after him or not. He ran until he made it back to his home in LaVoute, in Mizak. He ran to make it back to his family.

Francois later told me that it was actually in his classroom that the most people in the whole school died that day. He was lucky to have been one of the few survivors.

As I stood there three days after the quake and looked at the body of the young man in front of me, I wondered if maybe this young man had sat at the third bench that day.

My eyes slid from their gaze on this corpse and down past the other limbs, fingers, and toes undistinguishable from mangled rebar, and to the ground of the rubble filled courtyard. My eyes ran across the courtyard and over to the far wall where I noticed a large mango tree towering above the school graveyard. That must have been where Francoise jumped. Out in the street a motorcycle backfired and a group of pigeons scattered from the branches of the tree and flew off into the blue sky above towards the roof of a neighboring hotel. Their fluttering wings taking them farther away from death echoed the story of another friend of mine who had survived the collapse of that school. Tigo Pascal claims his survival was thanks to God who gave him wings to escape death that day.

Tigo, a motorcycle driver and mechanic from Mizak, was sitting in a French class of UNASMOH with his brother, Gaby, on the third floor of the building. They were going to have an exam that day in class which the professor had just handed out after having asked a few sample questions to prepare the students.

Tigo and Gaby were sitting on the same bench but with three other students in between them. The exam sheets had just arrived in their hands when they heard an earth shattering noise and felt the building start to tremble. Tigo thought that an airplane had fallen out of the sky and landed on the top of the building. He looked up and saw the wall in front of him start to fall towards him. He quickly crouched on the ground and hid under the bench in front of him. From under the bench everything turned dark and the air around him filled with dust. He couldn't see anything but he felt blood splatter on him from all directions as the noise consumed him.

"Gaby!" He yelled through the chaos. "Gaby! Are you there? Gaby?"

Gaby was there. When he felt the building quake he saw multiple students begin to run but he stayed sitting, not understanding what was going on. Then when he noticed the wall start to fall, instead of jumping under the bench like his brother, he jumped on top of it and vaulted himself off of it into the imploding world before him. Looking back he says it was like diving into the sea. "I felt as if the earth was swallowing me whole."

When he landed he sat still for a moment then heard his brother's voice coming through. "Tigo!" He called. "Tigo! Are you okay? Nothing fell on you?"

Tigo heard Gaby's response and started crawling towards him. He crawled over other bodies that weren't moving or crying for help. They were just bathing Tigo in blood as the collapsing walls mutilated them more and Tigo passed them quickly to get to his brother.

When Tigo reached Gaby he was relieved to see they were both okay, but they were still lost in darkness and unsure of where to go.

Then Gaby noticed a spot of light and pulled on Tigo's arm, "Let's go!"

They got up from the floor and darted towards the hole. Once up on their feet they saw what was going around them. They looked forward and saw their friend Peter just as a huge chunk of the wall fell directly on his leg and immediately cut it off. Peter fell over on the ground and lay there yelling. They ran over the wall that had just fallen on his leg and out of the hole into the open. There they could see that the entire building was toppling and they were falling towards the ground, but they weren't out of time yet.

A classmate behind them yelled to them from underneath a wall. They looked and saw his torso exposed and turned around to try to help him. The two of them tried to lift the wall off of him, but could not make it move. They couldn't do anything for that classmate, but then they saw Peter still lying there. They grabbed him and pulled him farther out where nothing would fall on him.

They felt an urge to try to save everybody around them, but they had to do something to save themselves. They left Peter there on the edge and they jumped to the ground. They were on the third story, but the first two floors had already collapsed by the time they got to the ground.

There on the ground Tigo sat and looked back and saw that the roof of the three story building that he had just jumped out of was now laying in a pile no higher than his head. He couldn't believe that he was alive sitting there to see it. He found out later that out of the 7 students that were sitting on his bench in the classroom, only he and his brother survived. As he sat there covered in dust, he remembered a dream that he had had the night before and began to understand.

In his dream Tigo was at his house when a police truck drove up and two policemen got out and rushed towards him and grabbed him. They yelled at him to get in the truck because they were going to arrest him. Beating him, they threw him in the back of the truck to take him down to the prison in Jacmel. In the back of the truck it was pitch dark and Tigo couldn't see anything, but the road was a lot worse than normal. The ride was extremely bumpy and he was being jostled around like a small child in the back of the vehicle. When they got to the prison the police opened up the doors and removed Tigo from the back. But at that moment Tigo decided that he was not going to allow them to throw him in prison where he could die so he jumped onto the hood of the truck and then on top of the roof. Once he stepped on top of the roof of the truck, wings suddenly grew out of his back and he rose up into the air and began to fly. He looked at the policemen below on the ground with the stunned looks on their faces and he went on into the air flying, flying, flying, until he made it safely back to his home in Mizak.

Tigo sat there now confident that he was meant to survive this disaster for a reason. "God gave me wings." He recalls.

Gaby was already on his feet and telling Tigo to get up too. Around them they saw many of the other students that were in the building now needing help and Gaby was ready to act. Both Tigo and Gaby drove motorcycles each day to class and Gaby told Tigo that that was how they could help. So they began finding those who were injured and putting them on their motorcycles to lead them to the hospital for help. Gaby first ran to see if he could find Peter. He found him there on the wall where they had left him, now fallen on the ground and lifted him up on his back and carried him to the motorcycle to take him to the hospital. He left him there in the yard of the hospital and went back for more as Tigo made rounds on his bike as well. They each made at least 10 trips back and forth that afternoon. Each time they would drive past dozens of other people with their own tragedies to confront in the streets, including Isabel Gere, Majorie's sister, who lived in the zone called Raquet near the hospital. As she stood there in the street before her toppled home mourning the loss of her baby, Tigo and Gaby would continue to drive by her and others unaware of the details of each individual story but knowing in the depths of their being they were intertwined at that moment nonetheless.

By the time that I stood there in the same courtyard where Tigo and Gaby jumped, on that Friday, they had received news that Peter had died waiting for treatment at the hospital.

I had stood there passing my eyes over this inexplicable tragedy for long enough. I decided that I had seen what I needed to see to confirm the stories and I didn't need to explore anymore. So I walked back outside and joined Berthony then we went into the main street to find another motorcycle to take us home. We were fortunate to find Berthony's cousin, and my good friend, Kenson, at the river with his motorcycle willing to take us back up the mountain without paying the outrageous prices that other taxis were charging.

Sitting on the moto on the way up, in between two of my best friends, Berthony and Kenson, I began to feel my usually positive, upbeat spirit sink and grow weak. I couldn't get the site of that body between the layers of cement out of my mind. I couldn't get that smell out of my head, out of my lungs.

We reached a point in the road about halfway up the mountain, a place called Nan Midi, where Kenson told us, "That's where I was." He pointed over to a huge rock bigger than a house and said, "I jumped off my moto and left it laying in the road to go hide over there behind that rock. I didn't know what I was hiding from. "

When we arrived back in Mizak, we returned to the house and found Julie who had just returned from visiting some families in the zone of Mizak called Sucrin who had lost a lot of young people in the cities during the quake. Julie was visibly discouraged after talking to these grieving families and she said, "Those of us that didn't die in the quake will surely die of heartache." With these words she summed up how the entire country was feeling at that moment.

That day my entire understanding of this disaster that I was a survivor of had just been dramatically transformed. I had known that after January 12th I would never be the same, but it was January 15th and what I saw and smelled that day that defined everything from that moment on. It was that day that I discovered where the stars had fallen.

ARTWORK BY PHOENIX JUNIOR BADIO

GOD IN THE CORNER

Not all of the stars that fell in Jacmel fell under layers of cement, however. Some fell into the sea.

An artist friend of mine who lives in the city, Phoenix Junior Badio, was sitting out in the back yard of his favorite gallery/bar at Hotel Florita when it all happened. This hotel is located in the arts district, just a few blocks south of the St. Michel hospital where Tigo and Gaby would transport their classmates. The hotel is known as a popular hangout for all of the city's creative types. Phoenix along with many of his colleagues and friends were relaxing out back as they frequently did, looking out over the sea before them across a beach known as Lakou (Courtyard) New York.

Before any of them felt anything one of Phoenix's friends pointed over to the shore. "Hey everyone, check that out," he said. They all looked over at the water and saw that the waves had stopped crashing and the sea seemed to have stilled completely. Phoenix rubbed his eyes and squinted at the water. "I'll admit I had been smoking a little," he told me. "I wasn't sure if it wasn't just the weed making me see things." But everyone that was sitting there was seeing the same thing and they were all proclaiming their confusion and astonishment. "We'd never seen anything like it." Phoenix said.

Then, a moment later, they began to feel the earth quiver beneath them. A few of them got up and cried, "Anmwey!" But they all kept looking at the sea. As the ground shook, Phoenix couldn't believe his eyes as the water beyond the beach actually separated in two and a line split open revealing the ground beneath as the water vibrated. As it shook, Phoenix saw fish begin to jump up out of the water and across the divide. The fish themselves were crazed and seemed to know that something was wrong. It was like the water was electrocuting them and they were jumping out to try to get away.

Then people from the shore who also saw the fish jumping and the dry land exposed, started running into the water with buckets and baskets and sacks and started grabbing the fish that were being shaken right out of the water. Phoenix remarked that these people didn't even seem to notice that the earth was quaking. All they saw were the fish free for the taking and they lost their good sense and scrambled into the water. By that time he had understood that it was an earthquake being unleashed, but the dozens of people he saw running into the sea didn't seem to acknowledge any danger in what was happening.

Then, just as suddenly as it started, the earth stilled again and the waters crashed in on themselves consuming the hungry fishermen and women. A large wave rolled in and washed the water up onto the shore arriving almost at Phoenix's feet where he still sat behind the hotel. As the water receded once more he saw a few people lying on the sand coughing and crying for help. But he knew that many more went in than what he saw come out.

What Phoenix had just witnessed was not even worth trying to wrap his mind around. At least falling cement can be understood through the laws of gravity, but what happened at Lakou New York that afternoon is just one example of the many things that occurred in those few seconds in this country that defied all explanation.

It wasn't worth trying to make any sense of it all. After having seen what I saw in Jacmel my own mind gave up on even trying anymore and began to surrender to the overwhelming senselessness. In this, I wasn't alone. Everyone went through the initial shock of the experience but then after having a few days to really think about it all and after the repetition of the aftershocks wearing away at our confidence, people started giving in to any wild conspiracy theory that would circulate. Nothing like this had ever happened in Haiti before so it was difficult to understand why it would now suddenly happen in such an extreme way. Also, after the witness accounts of the strange activity at the sea, it was hard to accept that something so unusual could be just part of nature. And, although everyone was saying a lot of things about God, it certainly couldn't be an act of God because he would never want to kill that many of his children, so it must have been something else.

The most popular theory was that the US (or some other affluent war-hungry country) was testing some sort of super power bomb in the ocean that caused the quake. It certainly stood to reason that people who had never been educated on earthquakes and had never experienced one in their country, and believe in a loving God who controls nature, would search for a different way to explain what happened. And considering the history of my own country and others it's hard to argue that they would not pick Haiti if they had to choose a country to sacrifice for the sake of military weapons testing. But still, the stories were upsetting and no one knew what to believe. Their faith in God is so strong that they were willing to blame anyone but him for this catastrophe. At the same time their faith in Americans and other foreign relations is so weak that it seemed almost too easy to place the blame on them.

This matter of faith, however, was one place where I found myself outside of the Haitian experience. My own faith in anything good at that point had been injured and left helpless without aid like so many of the Haitians who were still waiting for medical care at the doors of the few standing hospitals. For all of my effort, I couldn't find a way to believe in any sort of god in the middle of such an absolute mess.

That Sunday after the quake, Julie and Berthony asked me if I would go to church with them. I decided not to accept their invitation, just because I didn't want to hear one more opinion on God's role in all of it. Everyone in this country had been saying something different about what he had been doing that week and I just didn't want to hear it anymore. With so much conflicting noise about God, it's impossible to choose one supposed truth to believe. Some would say we just needed to pray, to talk to him directly, but every time I would try that another tremor would seem to come along which would make me think, "Seriously God! That's not the response I was looking for!" I was trying to believe that he knew what he was doing, but I just wished that I knew what he was doing because at that point it made no sense at all to me.

Eventually I came to the conclusion that maybe he wasn't doing anything at all. Maybe he's not doing anything. Maybe he did all he was going to do thousands or millions of years ago when he created this earth and now he's just sitting back and watching what happens. Maybe right now he's watching and crying. Maybe this isn't what he expected to happen at all and now we all need to be afraid that God, himself, is in danger of dying of heartache. Maybe he died of heartache long ago when we started shooting each other and dropping bombs willy nilly and allowing each other to starve and thirst and hurt. Maybe Friedrich Nietzsche was right and we killed God, now we're all just perishing left and right from a nature that's lost control of itself and there's no God left in heaven to care. Or maybe all of those who are perishing arrive in Heaven and say, "Here *I* am, where the hell's God?" And then Saint Peter tells them, "Oh he's here, his house is right down the road, but he doesn't accept visitors anymore and he doesn't sit on his throne anymore. He just sits inside his home in a dark corner and cries all the time. So, if you came here expecting to give him eternal glory, sorry, he doesn't feel like he deserves that anymore."

There were a lot of maybe's and a lot of searching, but very little discovering of comfort or answers. Belief in anything seemed unreachable. Many of the Haitian's claims seemed especially slippery to grasp as plausible. They would make it sound as if God exacted this catastrophe upon this population as a clear and intentional punishment. One of Julie's older daughters, Pascale had returned from Port-au-Prince and told me that the earthquake happened because "people sin too much." One of my Living Media co-founders, Kesnel, a motorcycle driver who had also seen Jacmel, shared a similar perspective. I was talking to him about how you would see one large building completely demolished causing multiple deaths, but then all of the adjoining buildings for some distance in all directions seemed absolutely untouched. I asked Kesnel how someone was ever supposed to comprehend such a thing. He replied, "God just reached down with his hand and chose what to break and what to save." I didn't say anything in response to him but I couldn't bring myself to believe such a thing. After all, my house was one that got destroyed while the next-door neighbor's didn't suffer a single crack, so that wouldn't speak too highly of God's opinion of me. And Haiti certainly isn't the only country full of sinners, so there was no reason for God to focus his wrath so specifically on this location at that time.

I like to search for the balance that resides in all things and this is where I found trouble in the time of the Grinder. For every action, a reaction. Wherever there's black, there's also white. Where there's good, there's evil. Light, dark. Belief, doubt. Beauty, ugliness. Life, death. In all things opposing forces exist to provide balance in all of nature. As an artist, it's always been the aspect of God as Creator that's interested me most. It is in those very first few phrases of Genesis in which I find the most conviction, "In the beginning, God <u>created</u>..." More than a Father, Lord, Savior, or any of the other things that they call this deity, it is the possibility of God to be a Creator that is the most believable to me. But in order for the universe to maintain equilibrium, where there is creation there must also be destruction. God, as the original Creator has to face the same reality that every artist must reconcile themselves to, that in order to create, you must also be willing to destroy, or at least accept destruction.

Sometimes I'll make a painting and then some time later I come to decide that that canvas and that frame would be better used as a different painting. So I cover the old painting with a new coat of primer and start all over. Art historians have examined works of famous artists such as Picasso, Van Gogh, and DaVinci, with x-rays and other techniques to find that they did the same thing. Underneath some of the world's most famous paintings were other rough drafts that the artists decided to abandon and redo.

In this sense, it was not so hard to imagine that God may have arrived at a similar decision to make. Not that he regretted making Haiti or was disappointed in it, but that he had lost control and earthly forces had ruined its potential to ever emerge as the beautiful creation that he intended it to be. He had created a beautiful land full of beautiful people, but the powers of man had destroyed the natural beauty and crushed the hopes of the people. The powers of man had sent the country into a hole that it would never be able to crawl out of without a new start. The Haitians were accepting God's decisions to exercise control. After all, he's an old man and he does what he wants. But I felt sorry for God having to see his work of art destroyed.

Now, whether it was an argument between Jesus and Satan, or because there was too much sin, or just because it was that moment that the tectonic plates decided to collide, the creation was destroyed and the raw materials were presented with the opportunity to start over. The canvas was now blank and prepared for new possibilities.

It was difficult at that point when everyone had lost family, friends, and homes, but Haitians had been given a chance to start over. Now it was in their hands to decide what to do with the blank canvas before them. God just went back to his corner to mourn and wait to see what the Haitians would do. Maybe he went back to his corner and prayed that the rest of the world wouldn't screw things up again.

This is how I would force myself to begin interpreting the things going on around me in order to find even the slightest suggestion of stillness. But it wasn't easy. Believing in anything at that point was a struggle, especially believing in oneself. Although I was physically healthy on the outside, the earthquake had shattered the mirror inside of me that reflected who I was truly was.

I felt just as stuck as those bodies between the layers of cement, as if my own will to do anything had been amputated. I would have liked to have helped. I went down to Jacmel expecting to be able to help and found nothing. All I found were some abandoned bodies to photograph. I had already been feeling utterly useless up in Mizak since the quake and thought for sure, as bad as things were in Jacmel, that I could find some way to contribute to the relief efforts there. I was here, there was work that needed done, and I thought that I could help somehow. I thought surely I would run into scads of foreign relief groups doing their part to help the country recover from this catastrophe. I thought there were probably plenty of people who could have used an extra translator or just an extra set of hands. I thought I'd find some white people in the street all wearing ugly, matching t-shirts and rubber gloves and I could ask them if they needed any help. But I walked all through that mangled city that day and saw one single white woman on a motorcycle taxi pass by. And I could tell that she was one of the regulars in Jacmel, because we're a pretty unusual breed and she belonged. She wasn't one of the flocks of people that swoop in after an emergency to bring short term aid that I was hoping to find and help out. It was being said that thousands of foreigners had descended on PAP in the few days prior but it seemed that none of them had made it into the south.

I understood that transportation was tricky at that point, and once someone arrived in Port-au-Prince and saw the need there, there would seem to be no reason to venture out any further. But I thought there had to be somebody, but Jacmel had become a ghost town. It seems that even the foreigners that were there before the quake hurried into PAP as soon as possible to focus their energy there instead. Especially after what I saw at St. Trinity I thought that surely there was someone wanting to do something about this. There was nobody. The site at the school was actually so abandoned that I could have done whatever I wanted there and even gone and walked all over the corpses without anybody to stop me.

I told the family at Julie's house that if I had the chance to go down and help remove bodies from the debris, I would have. I told them that I thought we all should have been willing to pitch in and help out at that time. We were just sitting around and that was what was needed right then, so why wouldn't I put on a mask and some gloves and start pulling hunks of house off of people, dead or alive? It would have made me feel a lot more worthwhile, personally. They all told me not to go. They all thought I was crazy for even being willing to go. So I asked them what I was supposed to do because I couldn't just sit and feel useless anymore. They handed me some ears of corn to shell for them. That defined for me my role in the situation. I knew that I wasn't there to be any sort of hero, but I was there to be a neighbor and friend. Those closest to me at that point didn't need lives saved, they just needed corn shelled.

I was torn between two worlds. I was a victim, plain and simple, even if a victim with different opportunities and privileges, yet at the same time, I was feeling the pressure from outside to be something more. This pressure was mostly coming from the United States, from the very people who were supposed to be supporting me. Every time I would talk to one of them it would just chip away at my fragile emotional infrastructure more.

Around that time I was at Paul's house one night when he handed me the phone to talk to a staff member from the US. "How are you?" I asked her to make conversation and be polite.

"Oh, we're hanging in there, but just barely," was her response. My own emotional insecurities at the time coupled with what I had recently witnessed in the city made me incredulous towards her comment. *She* was just barely hanging in there? I wasn't prepared to grasp the fact that others were going through different types of trauma even if they weren't in our shoes. Especially those such as this colleague who were so spiritually connected to the soul of Haiti but were not there physically during the quake, they certainly had their unique grief to deal with. But at that point, I was not in the mood to deal with hers over the phone.

She had no idea what it was like, I told myself, in an attempt to justify my rejection of her far-off suffering. No one had any idea. Those of us who had smelled the stench of rotting flesh that could have been our own and had it penetrate the deepest corridors of our souls knew this trauma on a much different level. Those of us who had shooed the flies away from our faces, the flies that were swarming around the dead. Those of us who had held the trembling victims in our arms, the ones so terrified that they can't form understandable words with their mouths. Those of us who had experienced the aftershocks, and had to wake up in the middle of the night to run for safety. Those of us who had to walk on the rubble, and sleep on the rocks and listen to the screams, and dry the tears, we knew something that no other souls could touch no matter how sympathetic. Everyone had a right to grieve, but trauma induced from watching the news on the television or the Internet, or even from hearing it on the telephone from a loved one is not the same as actually living the rancid nightmare and surviving.

At the same time, I realized that there were Haitians whose pain I could never imagine either even being there. I had heard their stories.

How people like Isabel Gere and Tigo Pascal even continued to function after what they had experienced seemed unfathomable to me at the time. There were so many survivors who could have very believably died of heartache, but they pushed on with strength and courage through a faith that tomorrow would be better. If someone asked them how they were doing, they wouldn't tell you that they're just barely hanging on. It was those Haitians who had the audacity to face each new day that I had to choose to be inspired by. Sometimes this also meant blocking out some of the questions from the states.

People would ask what I was doing and no matter what their intentions were I would interpret it as an accusation that I was doing nothing at all. I knew that I wasn't doing anything and I didn't need anyone else pointing that out for me. What I needed was someone to say, "It's okay if you feel useless right now, Lee, and need some time to just process everything. Things will get better soon." But no one was saying that. Instead I got questions about my activity and doubts about my commitment. Others present in the country chose to throw big "stress relief" parties with music and games, or hand out food to everyone in sight, or bandage wounds and give out pain meds, but it always seemed to be done mostly to appease the detached foreign donors and not because they were the most effective ways to help people. I just kept writing and communicating, believing in the power of the stories that were to be told. I continued to digest the entire experience but those things aren't so glamorous on the front page of the news.

It's incredible to see how quickly everyone becomes an expert on relief as soon as their heartstrings are tugged. I was receiving messages from churches back in Iowa as well, not of spiritual encouragement, but they suddenly had all of the answers to the country's problems. This is a sickness that we have as a race and as a nation, especially in the USA, that none are immune to, but a few grow to learn how to avoid giving in to the tendency. We wait until a disaster strikes then we flood the victims with perceived solutions that more often than not only complicate their recovery process. The church members back home couldn't resist the tendency. They were going to create houses out of earth bags and ferro cement and Styrofoam and pop bottles and grain bins. They were going to provide personal mobility devices for all of the newly handicapped Haitians. They were going to help provide new cooking systems and medical care and food aid, and of course they expected me to do all the grunt work on the ground to make it happen. And they wanted to do it NOW.

As much as I appreciated everyone's good intentions, as misguided as I saw them to be, it wasn't the right time to flood myself or the Haitians living the crisis with their grand ideas. At that point no one in the country was interested in experimenting with new technologies, they just wanted to get back to normal. They needed to get out of survival mode and just get back to living. If they could have gotten back to that point, and made up the ground that they lost January 12th, then they could worry about new ideas and advancing forward. But then everyone just wanted to get their heads back above water. Recuperate from the trauma first, and then begin to work on that blank canvas before them.

I continued to exist in an uncomfortable limbo caught between the humanitarian that everyone else expected me to be and the artist that I was created to be. Sometimes you just have to absorb the inspiration to understand it fully. Meanwhile, the earth continued to tremble, we continued to sleep outside under the stars, and the stories of what everyone lived continued to circulate.

ARTWORK BY ALEXANDRA AMAZAN

THE CAVE

A week after the quake I woke up to find some strange news that had saturated the community. Apparently in the zone of Mizak called Charlot, during the earthquake, a huge hole had opened up in the ground and deep inside under the earth you could see a wide range of artifacts from the slave days. Reports varied but we heard that you could see anything from jewels to tools from the plantations to Indian skeletons buried underground that had now become visible since the quake opened up the earth. I, of course, hurried to join the packs of pilgrims leaving their homes to go see what everyone was talking about. I was sure, as with any rumor that starts that way, that the accounts were undoubtedly embellished, but had to be based on some facts, so it must be worth going to see. It seemed to me, that if it turned out to be even partially true, then it would be a unique effect of the disaster to witness. It certainly seemed more interesting than hearing more about all of the people who had died to find that this act of nature had uncovered some long lost pieces of history.

So I headed out early with Papi and more people kept joining us along the way until we had a band of at least 25 curious Musacoise headed toward Charlot. My friends Zizi and Guy joined us, whom I hadn't seen since the day of the quake when they were both part of the crowd looking at my ruined house on the hillside. I asked where they had been and why I hadn't seen them. They had a different story to tell. Even though their experiences on the day of the quake were pretty typical for people in Mizak, in that week following the disaster they got involved in ways that would show them a completely unique perspective on the whole event.

They both are members of the Haitian Scouts that was called into the city immediately after the quake to help with security and other parts of the relief effort. They helped clear rubble from roads and handle crowd control at food and clothing distributions as well as help guide patients waiting to be seen at the hospital. They were helping the UN and the Red Cross and the Haitian government try to bring some immediate aid to the victims in Jacmel. They were the ones being the heroes while I shelled corn.

"We've seen a lot of people really lose their minds in some of these relief activities," Guy told me. At one event where they were handing out cooking oil, the UN was up on a stage to hand out the oil and the Scouts were down on the ground to control the crowd. But as soon as the boxes of oil arrived, the hundreds of people waiting to be served swarmed the stage and started ripping open the cardboard boxes and grabbing jugs of oil before the UN soldiers could even attempt anything organized. The Scouts were overpowered and couldn't do anything to control the people.

Then the Scouts even began climbing up on the stage just to remain safe. When Guy climbed up on the stage he realized that his tan Scout uniform was soaked in blood. He hadn't noticed getting injured and wasn't sure if the blood was his own or someone else's from the crowd.

"The UN couldn't do anything either," Guy said, "because they don't speak Creole. So it was up to those of us Scouts to try to tell the crowd of people that there was plenty of oil for everybody and they didn't need to fight. But they didn't pay any attention to us. Everyone was only concerned about themselves."

Sometimes an isolated fight would break out that would distract all of the UN soldiers and the Scouts as they would try to break it up which allowed others to sneak behind the stage and steal more oil. "It was complete chaos," Guy recalled as we walked. After things settled down he was able to confirm that he wasn't injured but couldn't tell who was either. Everyone was fending for themselves.

At another event they were invited to help hand out some clothes. "People didn't even need to know if the clothes would fit them or anyone in their family. They just started grabbing for whatever they could get." People would take anything because even if they didn't need it they could sell it later to someone who did and make some money. The Scouts tried to keep order, but again, it was impossible. People would take their share multiple times. Mothers would bring all their children and have everyone in the family take a share. There was no controlling the Haitians hungry for a handout.

"Then some people started throwing rocks," Zizi said. They threw them to scatter the crowd so that they could get to the front easier to take what they wanted. As soon as the rocks started flying, Zizi didn't know what to do, so he ran too. Someone stopped him and asked why he was running away when he was one of the ones supposed to be helping the situation. He told them that rocks don't have eyes and he wasn't going to be a victim.

I had talked to another friend just the day before who was in the crowds at one of these food distributions held in Jacmel. "They just threw the food at us like we were dogs," she said as she cried just thinking about it. "It was so humiliating."

Zizi and Guy responded to the call to come help clear the streets too. They spent almost three days in the arts district in the south of the city and around LaKou New York, where Pheonix and his friends saw the sea split in two, just moving rubble and debris from the area so people could pass through the streets again. "I didn't mind picking up the rubble in the streets," Zizi said, "but when they asked some Scouts to help remove rubble from some of the buildings that had bodies in them, I refused." At the St. Trinity School alone, Zizi had six friends of his, neighbors from Mizak, that died in the collapse and he didn't want to have to be the one to uncover them. "I spent the whole week down in the city and didn't see one body," he said. "I didn't want to see them. I could smell them the whole time when we were working in some areas, but I wasn't going to volunteer to go be the one to pull them out."

At the St. Michel hospital they were assigned another impossible job of trying to streamline the intake of patients and even perform triage to decide who needed help the most. Some of those patients included the classmates and teachers from St. Trinity that Gaby and Tigo had delivered on the backs of their motorcycles. The Scouts' job was made especially difficult because the buildings of the hospital in Jacmel were also severely damaged. The entire maternity unit had collapsed in the quake leaving only one survivor and multiple other sectors of the hospital had fallen creating victims in the very place that people were searching for healing. This left much of the work to be done under tents early on.

Guy and Zizi said that it was absolutely suffocating in those tents with so many people crowded in looking for help. Even the nurses and doctors on hand found it hard to breathe sometimes as they tried to work on patients. The Scouts tried to organize the people waiting to be seen outside, but each person, of course, thought that their medical need was the most urgent, making the Scouts' efforts even more challenging.

"Then I spotted one tiny, old lady in the middle of the crowd," Guy told me. "She had to be at least 100 years old. She was bent over and standing with a cane. She looked as if she couldn't even see and I was afraid that she might get trampled. It was clear that she was never going to be seen if someone didn't help her because all of the younger, stronger people who were pushing and shoving to get to the front would overpower her." So Guy walked up to her and tried to lead her to the front of the line, but she was so weak that she couldn't even walk. So he called over Zizi and the two of them picked her up, one at her shoulders and the other at her feet, and carried her straight to the doctor.

We continued towards the mystery cave in Charlot as Guy and Zizi shared their frustrated accounts of well-intended intervention. Their stories proved just how impossible relief could be when even the largest and most experienced of international organizations couldn't do it effectively. Not here, at least. Not at these moments.

"I was supposed to be in Port-au-Prince, you know." Zizi told me then. He had been going to school in the city and was just back to Mizak over Christmas break. He was supposed to return for school the week before the quake so that he could start classes on Monday the 11th. But when it was time to go back, his father didn't have enough money yet to pay for the second semester of school, so Zizi decided to stay in Mizak for an extra week to see if they could find the money that he needed to return.

"A lot of my classmates died in that school in Port-au-Prince," he said, his thoughts growing distant. Zizi questioned whether it wasn't God that kept his father from finding the necessary money.

By this time we had reached Charlot but although everyone in our large group had heard the reports, no one knew exactly where in Charlot to find the marvel. So once we arrived at a certain point we all stopped and sort of looked at each other unsure of where to make our next step. Pretty soon some local boy who had found us said, "It's over here!" Then he led us on an overgrown path and through a patch of thick bushes that opened up into a ravine over a small stream. But we all looked and saw nothing. Then someone else said, "I heard that it was in the caves in the cliffs down the river." So we all began following him.

When we arrived at the mouth of the caves, there was no one else there to suggest that it was any big attraction, but it did seem that if we were going to witness anything unusual, it could well likely be inside these caves. I was the only one with a flashlight, and also seemed to be the only one brave enough or stupid enough to explore the unknown, so I plunged in first. At first, Zizi was the only one to follow me and as we entered all of the others stayed behind, including Papi, yelling at us not to go in. But I was intrigued already and wasn't going to miss seeing whatever was inside. As we continued, a couple others decided to join us, Guy and one other man, but the rest stayed outside and thought we were suicidal.

Just a few steps inside was a large hole filled with bat droppings that seemed like it could swallow you whole if you put your weight on it so we jumped around it placing our feet on the solid edges. After that we started seeing all the diverging tunnels and connected rooms and we began to explore. We fought off bats that scattered as we advanced and searched in the darkness for reasons behind the rumors. We took every route we could find and eventually ended up at another exit that led outside so we figured that was it and went back. When we got back out we saw that the number of people had at least doubled and they were all arguing about what was inside. We told them that all we saw were a lot of empty alcohol bottles and some animal bones.

By that time a few local men had come along who actually knew something about the caves and were explaining them to the crowds. They made them sound absolutely infinite and said there were a lot of voodoo paraphernalia to be found that mystic practitioners had left there in recent times but they said nothing of the claims that we had all caught wind of regarding the slave and Indian artifacts. Now with these men as our guides, however, more people wanted to go in, so we returned with a new group of about a dozen. They led us through all the same places that we four had already seen, with the exception of one extra room we hadn't found that had a tiny doll inside. There was one other place inside that he told us we could go but it was more difficult to get to and you sort of had to slide down to descend into the other area. Zizi and I were ready to check it out. We wanted to see everything these caves had to offer, but everyone else was ready to head back. When we got back out Zizi and I almost returned to find that other passage but we knew we'd have 20 new people behind us again if we did and that would ruin the whole experience. So we resolved to come back another day with just a few people and dig deeper.

We headed back home, but apparently people kept coming to visit the caves all day long. We met people in the road headed that direction the entire walk back. And the rest of the day we kept getting reports from people returning to Mizak of having seen the same thing - some interesting caves but none of the items that we heard claims of. I never once heard anyone who could say they saw any of it with their own eyes.

It was neat; it just wasn't what we had set out to see. But what really got me was the fact that these caves had always been there, probably since the beginning of time. It seemed for the people of Haiti, though, that the beginning of time was only a week ago and now every adventure was a new exploration of life. That's what made these caves so alluring. They certainly started out as a simple story that got elaborated upon as it was passed around until it became so unbelievable that everyone decided all at once that they just had to go see this wonder. If someone had told me that morning, "Hey there are these really cool caves in Charlot that I've always wanted to see. Let's take a hike and check them out." I probably still would have gone along and then wouldn't have had any reason to be disappointed or left looking for more. I probably would have been very satisfied and even looking for ways to turn it into a tourist attraction. On that day we were just looking for more than bat droppings and a creepy Barbie. I think the whole community was just craving some sort of activity to distract them from all of the bad news, and this little field trip had done the trick. For a few short moments we were all allowed to wonder what laid hidden inside these cliffs rather than what laid buried beneath the rubble. For these moments we remembered that there was a world beyond the rubble, even if we couldn't completely get back to it yet.

That was the day that I began hearing it said, "God has put us in the grinder and started grinding us up."

Like corn or coffee, it was suggested that God was turning the handle until nothing remained except for powder. A fine dust that would always cover the land as a reminder of what once was. And years from now when curious ones examine deep beneath the surface and inside the dark caves of whatever becomes of this country, they will find this dust there as a haunting echo of the epoch when the Grinder started grinding.

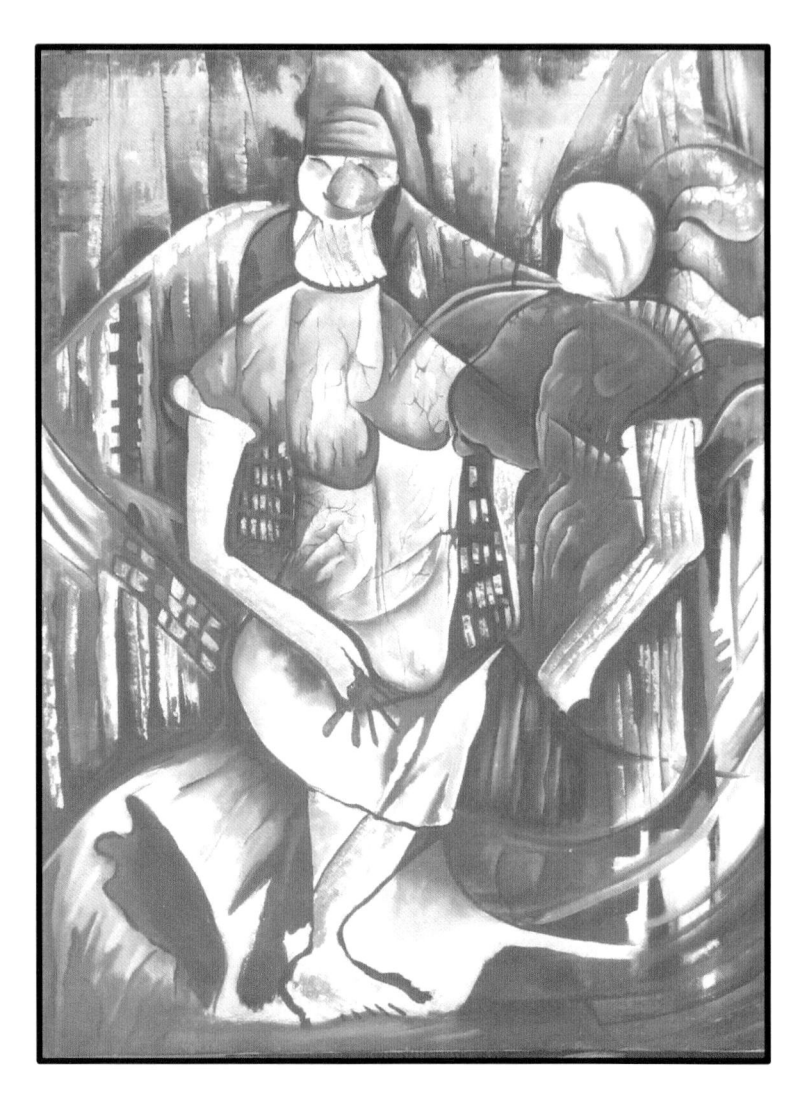

ARTWORK BY PIERROT CLERISSONT

STRANGERS AND BROTHERS

Within a few days my friends from Port-au-Prince started returning to Mizak, each one bringing a new perspective on the big picture of what this catastrophe meant. Pascale and Berline had already returned to Julie's house and a couple days later, older siblings, Nicodem and Gina joined the family too, each one of them sharing what they saw and what they lived. They brought news of other friends and family too. Nicodem told us of his good friend, Emmanuel Antoine, who had been injured in the quake and had been struggling to find care. Emmanuel's family lived in Kafou Sucrin, in Mizak, the area that Julie witnessed so much heartbreak over the number of young adults from there who had died in the cities. But Emmanuel was not one of the ones they lost. I knew Emmanuel well as a talented young man who had worked together with me on several community projects in Mizak before. He was someone that I really respected and was concerned to hear Nicodem's report about him but glad to have known he was alive.

Now with more available telephone service, I decided to give Emmanuel a call to see how he was doing. He told me that it was his foot that was injured and was not healing well. He didn't know when he would be able to make it back to Mizak because at that point he couldn't even walk. It was over three months later when Emmanuel actually returned to Mizak and I was able to sit down with him and hear his full story.

Before he started telling me his story, Emmanuel pulled up his left pant leg, exposing a large scar traversing his swollen foot and said, "The wound has finally closed, but I don't believe I will ever heal from what I experienced on the 12th of January."

He was in class at his university in Port-au-Prince at the time listening intently to his professor lecture before the classroom full of students on the fourth floor of the large concrete building. Class was almost over for the day with less than ten minutes remaining, when suddenly the lecture was interrupted by a deafening noise outside which Emmanuel thought seemed like a large tree that had been cut or had snapped and was plummeting to the ground. The sound scared the students enough that many jumped up and began to run, so Emmanuel did the same, but as soon as he rose to his feet he felt the entire building swaying in circles like a cornstalk in a cyclone. He lost his balance and found that he couldn't move. Then he looked up and saw large chunks of the wall begin to fall upon the students that were running to escape. Before he knew it they were falling on him too. One hit his left thigh and landed on his foot stripping off his pant leg and ripping open his shoe. He heaved the cement off with his hands and found the strength to move. Without thinking twice, he ran directly to the nearest opening that he could find, a window, and he jumped.

He jumped not to save himself, but because he didn't want to die underneath tons of cement.

What he didn't realize is that by the time he jumped, the lower two stories of the school had already collapsed on top of each other, so he didn't have as far to go to reach the ground as he thought. Once he landed, it took him a split second to realize that he was still alive. He heaved in a deep breath and felt his lungs take in the dusty air. He opened his eyes, still not understanding what was happening, and tried to get up to run, but his legs weren't able to take a single step and he fell back to the ground in pain. Again, he couldn't move. He couldn't do anything except lay there and watch as the school collapsed upon his friends, his classmates, and his teachers.

He lay there, stunned; not even attempting to understand what surrounded him. "I've never seen the city so black. The sky was a color of red that I've never seen with my eyes as if there was evil burning in the clouds. But underneath, nothing but darkness," he recalled. At 4:53 in the afternoon, Port-au-Prince was in mayhem, but Emmanuel saw nothing but blackness.

"I had no idea what was going on, but it didn't matter because I just needed to worry about getting myself to safety." He said that it seemed that was how everyone was in those moments following the quake. No one could help anyone else. Everyone was only worried about saving themselves.

As he looked around him, Emmanuel saw the street littered with rubble and bodies. Through the darkness, dust, and smoke, he couldn't tell which bodies were dead and which were clinging on to life like he was. He knew that he had to get away from where he was somehow. But everyone that passed by seemed to not even notice him suffering there. They were consumed with their own suffering. Then a tap-tap full of passengers drove by close to where he was laying and Emmanuel waved his hand desperately. He was fortunate that the driver noticed his signal and stopped the truck. The driver and another man from the back of the tap-tap got out and carried Emmanuel to sit him on one of the wooden benches in the back with the rest of the passengers. But with the roads full of debris and victims, the vehicle was not able to get far. After not even making it two blocks, the tap-tap could go no further.

The chauffeur waved down a policeman on a motorcycle and convinced him to take Emmanuel from there. The two men hoisted him on to the back of the motorcycle and the policeman took off with him weaving in and out of dust-covered Haitians crying as they walked.

They arrived at the L'Hopital General, the city's largest, and the country's only, public hospital, where the policeman was going to leave Emmanuel to get treatment. When they arrived, however, the hospital yard was packed with victims in search of help and they overflowed out into the street for more than a block. Emmanuel saw that he was not the only one in need of help. He looked around the mass of humans and saw that many of them were missing body parts completely. Some without arms or legs, others missing entire parts of their face or flesh off of their torso, and women who had their breasts torn from their chest. He saw people lying on the ground and others tossed in wheelbarrows all wailing in tortured cries to God above. He then looked up past the sea of agony at the hospital building itself and noticed that it too was injured like the victims before it with walls fallen and twisted. He then looked back down at his own scraped leg and mangled foot and knew that it was no use waiting for help there at L'Hopital General.

The policeman who was still with him on the motorcycle agreed and so they left and drove to the nearby public park which they call Champs Mars. Here they came upon an even larger gathering of people all having fled their homes to arrive here at the big open space, the only place that seemed safe without any buildings on it to threaten them. This is where the policeman left Emmanuel to fend for himself with the rest of the people from all over the city who were all trying to comprehend the same tragedy.

With the park already packed with people, Emmanuel got down across the street in the only bare spot he could find, the gutter. He descended onto the cold dirty street and settled into place and for the first time that afternoon, allowed himself to actually think. From the time that they heard the snapping sound in class, there had been no time for thought, only action, if he wanted to live. Now, even though he was far from finished with his journey, he felt safe there in the gutter amongst the thousands of other refugees. He thought about his family and wondered how they were and knew that they would be wondering the same about him. He knew that he had to find them somehow if he wanted to get home. That was the moment that he realized where his telephone was, in his backpack, under the rubble of his school building. He surrendered to the fact that there was nothing he could do.

As he relaxed he also realized that his head was in a lot of pain as well. He felt the right side of his scalp with his hand and felt a significant wound there that he hadn't even noticed through all of the chaos. He looked at his hand to see it covered in blood. He didn't remember if debris had fallen on him, or if it happened when he jumped, or somewhere else along the way. So he took his t-shirt off and tied it around his head to bandage the wound. He had a green handkerchief in his pants pocket that he took out and tied around his injured foot. Thinking that that was all he could do for now, he surrendered also to the fatigue that was overwhelming his body. He closed his eyes to the sounds of the masses singing and praying to God, and fell asleep.

Hours later he awoke to the same sounds of prayer and praise from the park. He didn't know what time it was but it was not yet morning. He looked down at his foot to see that his green hanky had turned red as it became soaked with blood. He noticed that the rest of his clothes were wet too, but they weren't red with blood. He smelled himself and realized that he was soaked in the urine and feces of the many people who were there on Champs Mars without any toilets and were using the gutter to relieve themselves. He tried to shift himself into a better position but it was too painful to move. So he just laid back down and looked up to see a boy a few feet above him unzip his pants and add to the stream of waste flowing onto his immobile body. He tried to fall asleep again, but by that time Champs Mars had become so crowded that the streams of people passing by kept stepping on his wounded foot. Emmanuel was too weak to even protest.

When the sun finally started to come up to prove to Emmanuel that he would, in fact, see another day, he decided he must do something to find his family. He got the attention of a nearby man and asked if he could borrow his phone to try and call his sister.

"It wouldn't do you any good," the man's response came, "communication has been blocked ever since the quake hit yesterday."

"None of them know that I'm alive." Emmanuel told him. "I'm sure they think I'm dead. Everyone else at my school is."

The stranger asked which school he was talking about. When Emmanuel told him, the man was stunned. "I walked by that place yesterday. I can't believe you're alive either." He said. Then he introduced himself, "I'm Frisnel."

Frisnel pulled Emmanuel out of the gutter and sat him on the concrete walkway and then sat down next to him leaning against a lotto booth as Emmanuel recounted his story and explained how he arrived to be where he was. Frisnel had his own story to tell as a fellow university student at a school nearby Emmanuel's. He too was in class at the time that the quake struck but was able to escape unharmed.

Frisnel didn't know anything about his family either, but by this time he had formed a new brother and was committed to helping Emmanuel however he could.

Emmanuel looked back and recalled, "Even though in the early moments after the quake everyone was only concerned about themselves, things soon began to change once we began to realize that we needed each other if we were ever truly to survive. It was that first night and the following days in which we as Haitians became more unified than ever before. Too many of our friends, family, and neighbors had already died. We began fighting to make sure that we didn't lose anymore. We started reaching out to one another."

"We've got to get you up and find your family," Frisnel told him. So he bent down and placed his shoulder under Emmanuel's left arm and wrapped his arm around Emmanuel's torso and gripped him tight as he raised him to his feet. Emmanuel put all of his weight on his new brother and Frisnel began to drag him through the masses of people.

With every step Emmanuel grimaced in pain and tried to hold back the tears. They hadn't even made it to the other end of the park when Frisnel looked at his face and noticed his suffering, "We can't do this," he said, and he sat Emmanuel gently down on the ground once again.

"Just leave me," Emmanuel said, "go find your own family. You don't have to do this for me."

"It's a miracle that either of us is alive right now," Frisnel told him. "I'm not going to leave you to die now. Just wait here," he said.

Emmanuel had no choice.

Ten minutes later Frisnel returned with a bicycle that looked like it had been pulled out from under the rubble itself. The owner of the bike that was willing to loan it to them came with Frisnel and the two of them together pulled Emmanuel up and the owner supported him while Frisnel got on the seat. Then he propped Emmanuel up in front of Frisnel and they wobbled as Frisnel started to peddle. They moved slowly through the people and finally made it through the masses that had gathered at the park. The bike owner jogged behind them.

They started moving faster but then realized that the bicycle had no brakes. Frisnel put his feet down and skidded to a rough stop causing Emmanuel to cry out in pain. "This isn't going to work either," Frisnel said, discouraged.

He got off and held Emmanuel under the arms once again and returned the bike to the owner who was just catching up to them. By that time, however, they had gotten near an important intersection of the city called Portail where they knew they could find a motorcycle. "Just hold on a little bit further," Frisnel said, and began to drag him once again. Emmanuel surrendered, once again, and ignored the torture that his body went through as they moved forward. He knew that it was his only chance to get home.

As they approached the intersection, they saw that they were not the only ones trying to get a motorcycle. Hundreds of people, most with injuries of varied degrees, were all there trying to get anywhere but where they just came from. They were all trying to find their ride out of hell.

The motorcycle drivers knew exactly how desperate everyone was to find that ride. Chauffeuring the tortured out of hell can be a very profitable business. Frisnel waved one down and told him that Emmanuel needed to get to the section of town called Martissant. The driver told them it would be 200 gourdes. "That's ridiculous!" Frisnel shouted at him. Emmanuel agreed. He usually made that same trip on a motorcycle for 10 gourdes. The driver rolled his eyes and tried to explain how the price of gas had skyrocketed in the last day since the quake and they wouldn't be able to find a ride for less. Frisnel didn't believe him and told him to go ahead on his way.

Then he waved down another driver and they received the same story. 200 gourdes. Frisnel sighed. Emmanuel moaned, knowing he couldn't wait much longer. No matter where he was going, or how much it was going to cost, he had to get there soon. They were able to negotiate down to 150 gourdes with this chauffeur and they hoisted Emmanuel on the back of the bike.

"I have no mouth that can tell you "thank you" enough." Emmanuel told Frisnel.

"It was no problem," came Frisnel's calm reply.

With that the driver kicked to start up his motorcycle's engine and they drove off. Unable to support himself, Emmanuel allowed his still bandaged head to lean forward and rest on the driver's shoulder as they wove through the rubble and people in the streets.

As the victims and collapsed buildings blurred by Emmanuel's eyes he silently rejoiced inside knowing that he would soon be with his family. He couldn't imagine where he would be if God had not sent his angel Frisnel to be his crutch, his guide, and his hope. He would probably still be laying in the excrement in the gutter. But now, he was on his way to reunite with his family.

As they pulled up in front of Emmanuel's sister's house in Martissant, Emmanuel pulled the 150 gourdes out of the pocket of his torn pants and feebly handed it to the driver. The driver pocketed the money, and then held Emmanuel up as he got off himself and then helped his passenger to the ground.

Knowing that Emmanuel could not stand on his own, the driver held him up and called inside the house, "Is anybody here?"

With that, Emmanuel's sister popped her head out of the doorway and immediately began to cry, "Mesi Jezi! Mesi Jezi! Anmwey!"

She ran, took her brother in her arms, and wept. The moto driver turned and left. And for the first time, in his sister's arms, Emmanuel surrendered to the emotion and wept himself. "I'd been holding back so much," he recounted, "at that point, I just let the tears flow."

The rest of the family heard the noise and ran out too, all embracing their brother who they thought had died. They saw he was injured and were worried by all of the random pieces of clothes that were bandaging his body, but there would be plenty of time for explanation and stories, at that moment they all just held each other and cried.

When the family did finally find themselves asking questions, they immediately began discussing how they were going to find some medical care for their brother. Emmanuel explained how he had passed by the hospital and what he witnessed, so they had to try to find other options. They had a neighbor who was a private doctor, but there were mixed feelings on asking him for a favor because he, himself, had just received news of his father dying in the earthquake. However, they knew that they had to try.

Despite his own loss, the neighbor agreed to help out Emmanuel. He gave him three shots, some pills, and bandaged up his foot better that had been tied with the handkerchief.

And although it seemed to take away some of the pain, the foot remained severely swollen. The next day there was another doctor who was walking through the street treating victims. When Emmanuel's sister saw him, she called him in to the house to look at the foot. He said that it needed to be drained. Nicodem was there and he took Emmanuel's hand as the doctor took out a scalpel. But with no anesthetic, as the doctor began to puncture the skin to let the blood out, Nicodem got weak and turned away, unable to watch. Emmanuel didn't cry and he didn't make a sound, but he squeezed Nicodem's hand as hard as he could while the blood flowed. The doctor wiped off his scalpel, put it back in his bag, and left to see who else he would find along the way.

Over the next couple of days, the foot only seemed to get worse. It swelled up even more and began to turn green. By that time some doctors had begun entering the country from the other half of the island, in the Dominican Republic. One of these doctors was a friend of Emmanuel's sister-in-law. She came and drained the foot once again, and gave him even more medicines.

"That's when it finally began to heal," Emmanuel said. But it was still more than two months before he could walk on it.

Then as I talked to him months later, the foot was still visibly swollen and he said he still felt pain inside. "But the pain gets less and less every day; though the memories remain as if it had happened yesterday."

Just as I finished talking with Emmanuel, his phone rang. "Alo...Oh, Frisnel! How are you, my friend?" I looked at Emmanuel and raised my eyebrows as if to ask, "is that who I think it is?" He just smiled and gave me a nod as he shook my hand. He got up, walked away, still with a slight limp, and chatted with his new good friend that God brought into his life, to save his life from the Grinder.

ARTWORK BY JOHNNY GABRIEL

SATAN IN THE STREETS

Emmanuel may have said that he encountered an angel that day, but angels weren't the only spiritual beings present during that time. The competition between Jesus and Satan continued in the streets even after those first tumultuous moments. Everyone may have been calling Jesus' name as soon as the earth stilled, but Satan wasn't going to let him win that easily. He still had a few tricks up his sleeve as well. He knew how to use fear to influence this society because he had been doing it for centuries before the quake.

Monsters and demons have always been more than just Mardi Gras costumes in Haiti. Ever since I had moved to the country I had heard my Haitian friends talk about them. There are many different words in Creole for these creatures of hell, each with a slightly different meaning. "Dyab," "lougarou," and "zonbi," are some of the most common and most feared ones. I had learned these words well as I had been warned about them and told of what they could do.

My roommates wouldn't even let me go outside at night to urinate because it was too dangerous with the beasts lurking about. They were used to living with buckets and vases and tubs under their beds to take care of their needs in the middle of the night because ever since they were little kids they were taught not to tempt the dyabs by wandering outdoors at night, even for a moment. I kept my skepticism intact but also tried to remain open minded towards a belief that this culture had engrained into the minds of its people. I was not, however, willing to adapt to the culture to the point of peeing in a vase at night. From the first night that I spent in Haiti I discovered this. With boys especially, it's noisy, there's splattering, and then there's the issue of someone having to take care of it in the morning.

So with my friends who decided to live with me, we came up with a compromise and decided that we would just take a group potty break every night. The dyabs are less frightening in groups. So every night, whoever would wake up first would then wake the rest of us up and we would go outside together to relieve ourselves. Even then, no matter how badly one of us may have to go, we were still never in a hurry. Whoever was first would still always pause after opening the door and listen carefully and look around before stepping outside. And on more than one occasion it was in fact decided unsafe to venture outside and we all had to just hold it until morning. Then, the next morning, after the sun had come out, the guys would explain to me why. They would tell me that they had heard a suspicious nonhuman noise or even smelled a deathly smell and we couldn't take the chance. It was early on while studying the spirits and principalities that control the night in this country in relation to their threat level to my nightly urination that I began to form a sympathy towards my friends' superstitions.

After the earthquake on January 12, 2010, however, these lougarou seemed to take control of the land like a foreign army occupying the country. They seemed to be aware that the population was now so terrified of falling walls that they laid in the open like a smorgasbord of human life ready to be consumed. They seemed to have awakened from their slumbers and crawled out of the very cracks in the earth that the quake opened up so that they could terrorize the population even further. Satan was committed to reminding the Haitians just how frightening he could be. Nowhere was this more apparent than in the capitol city.

Port-au-Prince was already the most miserable place on the planet before January 12th, but the chaos caused by the earthquake plummeted the city into a completely unearthly atmosphere altogether. The aftermath of this disaster gave birth to a hell that no one could ever imagine. Those fortunate enough to still be able to walk and move were able to escape.

Tigo and Gaby Pascal went straight into the city the morning after they survived the collapse of St. Trinity to search for their sisters. They had five sisters living in the capitol plus two brothers, and without phone connection, they hadn't heard any news from them yet so the two of them decided to drive there and see with their own eyes if their family was okay. They took the same road into the city that Rodrigue Badio had traveled by foot to escape and they had to frequently create their own routes as the main road was blocked in many places by fallen rocks and rubble from broken buildings. As they passed through Leogane and entered the city, however, the obstacles changed and they had to start weaving around the bodies lying in the streets with their motorcycles. After having the blood of victims splattered on himself only hours before, Tigo said that it was nearly impossible to see those bodies in the streets and drive by as if they weren't there at all. "But we were so focused on our seeing our little sisters that we had to pay no attention to all of the death that we were driving through. It was like there were just a lot of rocks in the road. We had to find our family."

They did arrive to find all of their siblings safe but in a hurry to get out of the city. They all fought over who would get the places on the motorcycles to go back to Mizak immediately. None of them could wait to get out of the situation they were in. They took their four younger sisters, and the others agreed to wait until they could find other transportation.

At the same time there were many people like Emmanuel Antoine, who were stuck there in Port-au-Prince to experience the suffering and fear that boiled in those rubble-strewn streets. "I wanted to get out of there so badly," Emmanuel recalled, "especially after days of not finding the medical help that I needed, but my injury wouldn't allow me to leave."

It was in those days that the reality of the spiritual war between good and evil that had always been engaged over this country reared its ugly head in full force. It was in those days that it seemed evil would win. Every living soul in the capitol at that time witnessed the battle in the streets in at least one form or another.

Nicodem and Gina had only spent a few days there before they decided to retreat to their home in the countryside, but those few days were enough for them to witness the horrors of an entire city possessed by fear and uncertainty. With everyone sleeping in the streets and open parks, when the light of day would fade away, bands of hungry demons would creep out and take to the streets searching for helpless victims to prey upon. When the dyabs band together like this, together with the zonbis raised from the dead, they also find people so terrified of death that they surrender and allow themselves to become possessed to join the unearthly army. In Creole, this army of terror is called "regiman" and it is the most feared entity in Haitian belief.

I had heard stories of regiman already from my friends in Mizak, how they don't even need to be nearby to devour you. They could be miles away, if they hear you sniffle or even smell your scent, in an instant they can surround you and absorb you into their evil band. You have no time to escape and if you resist, you die.

When Nicodem and Gina returned to Mizak, though, they told us of how the regiman had taken control of the night in the city. Huge groups of unearthly creatures and the demon possessed humans, naked and wild, would swarm the streets and snatch babies and small children from under their mothers' arms. Every morning when people would wake up they would seem to find more bodies in the streets than the day before, not people who died from earthquake injuries, but people who had been killed by the spiritual forces of the night.

"When you hear them coming, there's nothing you can do." Nicodem told us. "The men grab their machetes and the women pray."

Gina said, "We're afraid to go into the streets during the day because the streets are still full of bodies and there are so many criminals loose from the damaged prisons. We're afraid to go into the streets at night because of the dyabs and regiman that want us dead. We're afraid to go inside our house because the walls are cracked and the aftershocks continue. We're afraid to stay outside because of the rain that has started falling. Fear has left us nowhere to go."

It was such a relief when these friends started showing up in Mizak after the quake. We had known that they were all alive, but as long as they were still in Port-au-Prince no one could be sure what was going to happen to them because that city was still full of so many fatal possibilities. So being able to see them and hug them was confirmation that they were going to be alright. Even though at that point Mizak may not have been Paradise, these friends had at least made their way out of Hell.

They weren't the only two though. Many friends were coming back from the capitol little by little and each one of them brought with them more stories of the devil's activities in his hell on earth.

One of these friends, Dominique Michel, recalled how much more careful you had to be if you crossed the path of certain animals in those days. The spirits of the undead would find the body of an animal to possess. If you were out after dark and came across a cow, a donkey, a turkey, a dog, or any other animal that was loose and walking freely in the street, you could be sure that it was more than just an animal.

Dominique said that after the earthquake especially, if you saw an animal acting strange at night you couldn't be sure what it was. It could be an actual dyab that had possessed the animal to search for people to eat and chaos to cause in the streets, or it could just be someone who was stuck under the rubble who had powers in these mystic matters. They could send their spirit onto an animal in an effort to escape too.

I asked Dominique what he would do if he did see one of these animals. He told me that he would just avoid it but sometimes if the animals truly get out of control and do create destruction and threaten people then a voodoo priest or priestess must be called. "They have to find someone who is more powerful than the spirit that inhabits the animal. Then that person will communicate with the spirit and take measures to control it so that it will submit and stop what it's doing. Sometimes this hougon or mambo will actually have to mount the animal and ride it back to its house where they have to beat and torture it. In the morning the person whose spirit had possessed the animal will be found dead and the animal will be fine."

It was these sorts of extreme measures that had to be taken in that time after the first trembling to protect the population from the evil tendencies that raged in the cultural aftermath of the natural disaster.

Daniel Prevot knew of a woman, a neighbor of his in the city, who encountered a regiman unexpectedly one night when she had left the market a little too late and didn't make it home before dark. While walking back to her house she passed through a small deserted alleyway. She was alone with her basket of goods from the market on her head, and could see very little through the faint glow of distant streetlights. She noticed another person walking in the opposite direction towards her and began to walk a little faster. But as she met the other figure it stopped in front of her and blocked her from going any further. "Eksise'm?" She said softly, politely requesting permission to pass, but the individual made no movement and no sound.

She looked at the person and noticed that it was a man and he was looking intently at her with dark eyes. As she met his gaze, she was transfixed. Then, without warning, she was surrounded by at least 20 figures encircling her and crowding the small alleyway. She didn't notice how or when they appeared but she was trapped by them and couldn't get away. She tried to scream for help, but felt her voice disappear. The creatures in her midst, whether human or other, were making noises, almost as if they were speaking to each other, but she didn't understand anything they said.

She became dizzy and passed out.

The next morning she found herself in her bed at her home feeling extremely ill. She told her story to her family and friends who came to visit her. Daniel was good friends with her son and saw her two days after the incident. He said she wasn't herself. She seemed very confused and could talk about nothing else but the dyabs. She was clearly in great physical pain at the same time and she was getting worse each day.

Five days later, she died.

Just the emotional effects of what people witnessed on that day in Port-au-Prince could send many into a sort of hell within their own minds. My friend Choumimi is a police officer in the city and some of his accounts in particular paint pictures of a carnal place too dreadful for human life. Because of his position, he was confronted with atrocities unlike anyone else.

On the afternoon of the 12th when it happened he was sitting with some friends in front of their house, after a day of working at the station, in the zone of Martissant. After the earth stilled he remembers the confused moments as everyone tried to confirm life. These couple minutes were filled with the most absolute silence that he had ever heard before the whole country erupted with their single unison cry to Jesus.

Choumimi got up from where he was sitting and walked through the crying masses to the nearby police station where he had been working just earlier that day. He arrived to find the station building critically damaged but still standing. His fellow officers were all standing around sharing their disbelief in what had just occurred. Choumimi joined his comrades talking about the situation that was evolving around them. As they stood there exchanging perspectives, all at one moment the talking stalled and all heads turned towards the entrance of the station and all eyes fixed upon a woman walking in.

"She was a woman," Choumimi said, "That much we could tell." But beyond that the woman was unrecognizable. Her body was charred black with patches of bright pink muscle exposed in places through the disfigured flesh. Her clothes had been burnt off and she looked "like a human turned inside out and rolled in charcoal." She had just walked over a kilometer from the gas station in the main road which had exploded in flames leaving dozens of victims dead. It was this same gas station that Rodrigue Badio would soon walk by as he escaped the horrors of the city on foot to return to Mizak. This woman had survived the explosion and by some miracle was able to walk to the police station where she was hoping to find help. What was even more unbelievable to Choumimi and the other officers was that she could speak.

"She begged us to help her," Choumimi recalls, "but none of us there could do anything." The one pick-up that they had at the station just had a large chuck of a wall fall on top of it and was not drivable. Even if they did have a vehicle the roads were impassable and there was no way that they could get her to a hospital. Even if they could get her to a hospital, the police had already received reports of the situations at the hospitals of how they were damaged themselves and immediately maxed out in capacity and unable to help people coming in. Even then, Choumimi, and everyone else standing there looking at this woman knew that even if they could get her immediately to a quality hospital before the most talented doctor in the country, there was absolutely nothing that any human being could do to save that woman.

She pleaded desperately with them, her mouth slurring the words with a swollen tongue through a lipless hole in her face. She cried before them, her eyes unable to form tears, bulging out from rigid sockets with a thin layer of flesh melted to them. A claw like hand blistered and frail reached out and touched one officer's arm searching for hope. The officer recoiled unintentionally, then realized what he had to do and took her by the shoulder to lead her outside.

"We all felt horrible," said Choumimi. "We are the national police. We are the ones who are supposed to be able to help our country's citizens in any situation. But at that moment there was nothing that we could do. The woman had no choice but to die."

As I heard these stories I was thankful that if I was going to have to live through an experience such as this I was living through it in Mizak. Mizak, however less terrifying than Port-au-Prince, still wasn't immune to the evil.

After our first couple nights of being nomads sleeping on random rocks in the community, Berthony, Sony, and I settled in at our friend Astrel's house where they had a nice little patch of soft grass under their almond tree in the front yard. Here the family had set up a shelter from tarps and sheets where they were sleeping and they accepted the three of us to join their commune. Their home was very near the rocky hillside where Berthony and I had slept for a couple nights but at least we felt like we were inside something. The hibiscus bushes created a nice barrier to the outside and the random pieces of fabric and plastic completed the walls. Here at least we didn't feel so exposed to whatever beings may wander in the dark. It was here that we slept every night for two weeks while we were still trying to gauge the stability of the earth.

It was here under the almond tree that we felt safe sleeping for a while, but it was also here that I experienced some things that severely contradicted my American skepticism towards the Haitian superstitions. I had always been able to apply reason to justify my doubt of my friends' claims of dyabs, but life in the Grinder defied all reason.

One night we had been lying there on the grass for a couple hours just talking and telling jokes as we did each night before falling asleep. We were all laughing and enjoying ourselves as Astrel's goofy 6-year-old brother was dancing and entertaining us to his self-invented rap beats. Then suddenly Astrel's mother gasped loudly and started quieting everybody down. "Shhhhh..." She said intently but without saying any words. "Shhhhh...."

I heard everyone subject to a necessary silence but I wasn't getting the hint. "What? What's going on?" I was saying. "What are we listening for?"

Berthony shot me a glare that said, "Just shut up!" with his eyes. I did. And I listened, but I was not hearing anything. Everyone else was obviously aware of something that I could not discover with my limited American senses that were untrained in these things.

It was a couple minutes later when I did finally hear a noise approaching. It wasn't footsteps. It wasn't human. It was a low roaring noise and it was coming closer. We all lay as still as could be and were afraid to even breathe. Astrel's mother held her youngest son tight and put her hand over his mouth. The noise was coming from some sort of being that was passing by in the path just in front of the house. This being was passing, but not walking. I could not hear feet stepping on the ground but rather a rumbling vibration. The path crossed in front of the yard no more than three feet from where my head lay on the grass. As the creature passed on the other side of the hibiscus bushes, we all lay petrified and I felt like I could hear it breathing. The noise was so unlike anything I had ever heard, finding words to describe it seems impossible. It seemed like a steady intense moaning, but it did not seem to be coming from a mouth of anything. It just floated by and reverberated in our souls.

A moment later it was gone but no one moved. I was sure that just the same as when it came, everyone else was still aware of it even though I couldn't hear it anymore. Another couple minutes passed and I looked over at Berthony again who was lying next to me. He returned my gaze, but this time his eyes said nothing. In them was a mixed sense of fear of what just occurred and relief that we all were still there. We all remained there, just as we were, without making a sound, until eventually we all fell asleep.

The next morning I knew better than to even ask questions. I knew that I'd get a response like, "It was a lougarou, you moron!"

A few nights later I had woken up with a full bladder. Out of habit, and fear of the lougarou we had heard before, I woke Berthony up to see if he would go pee with me. After a moment of stillness to make sure nothing was lurking about, we both got up and stepped outside just on the other side of the path to take care of business. We were facing the east and just after getting started we caught a glimpse of a bright light emerging off to the north. I turned my head slowly to see what it was and I saw Berthony to my left do the same.

On top of the rocky hillside nearby, where we had slept several days earlier, we noticed a small fire burning on the ground. But almost immediately it started to grow. It grew up, not out, straight up until within only a few moments it was the height of a human being, but no wider than a couple feet. At that Berthony grabbed my shoulder and pulled me back without enough time to even arrange myself from what we were doing. We jumped back behind the hibiscus at the entrance to Astrel's family's yard and stayed there to watch what this fire would do. From where we were at a distance it was hard to tell exactly how tall it was, but it seemed to me now about ten feet tall.

It was impossible for me to understand. It seemed like something that could only be created by special computer effects in a movie. It was a huge pillar of fire that suddenly grew out of the rocks.

Then, as we looked at it, if it wasn't hard enough to understand already, it began to move. It floated across the hillside heading east away from us. It was as if a human had been set on fire and was now walking completely unaware that they were burning. Yet it moved slowly and intently. It was just a tower of fire out for a stroll at midnight in the countryside. As it moved it passed behind trees and then down the hill until it was only a glow and then it disappeared in the distance. I stood there and stared but Berthony took my arm and said, "Let's go back to bed."

That morning after, I had to ask Berthony for confirmation to make sure that it wasn't a dream. Berthony retold me what he saw, exactly the way that I had seen it. Although my interpretation was still riddled with foreign attempts at logic and reason whereas Berthony had been sensitized to these sorts of things since birth, so his memory was even more colorful still. Nonetheless, it was undeniable. It was inexplicable. It was frightening.

That was how life was at that time. And now I share these stories fully aware that I may come off as seeming a bit crazy to those who've never witnessed such things. I also share them with the conscious admission that I was, in fact, somewhat mentally unstable at that time. But I know what I saw and heard and felt. I also must admit that these are only two of multiple instances in this country where I have had such strange even otherworldly encounters. I can't explain them, but I still must share them.

Some psychologists could probably analyze it all in a much different way, but it seemed like, in those days especially, everyone in Haiti had just witnessed so much death in such a sudden moment of time, that we became more sensitive to the after-death that surrounded us. We had lost all reasons to believe in what was natural because nature had betrayed us. Now the supernatural became more evident. People looked to God for answers and peace, but that doesn't mean that they forgot about Satan, becoming even more acutely aware of his activity. Sometimes believing in the capacity of Evil seemed the only way to survive it.

ARTWORK BY ASTREL JOSEPH

MEETING JESUS

Another friend of mine, whose story I also did not hear until months later, reaffirmed the presence of Jesus in it all through her experience. After living through her own unique tragedy, she says she met Jesus on a pick-up truck. But it all started earlier somewhere very unexpected. The Goudougoudou of January 12th caught everyone somewhere different, in the street, in the kitchen, or in the field. It caught Eveline Louis in the shower, bathing.

She had just returned from school and was at a friend's house where she frequently stayed in the Kafou district of the capitol city, the same district where Rodrigue Badio went to school, nearby her own home that she rented with her three other sisters. Her friend was preparing supper and setting the table for some guests, which included a pastor, and Eveline decided to take a quick shower before eating. She was just finishing up and taking a final rinse off when she heard a loud noise that she thought was someone jumping from rooftop to rooftop above her. As she poured water over her she yelled up above her, "Who's there running around on the roof?" She wiped the water from her face and looked up to see that the buildings themselves were shaking. "Anmwey!" She cried and grabbed her panties and pulled them on as she ran out of the shower.

She was in between houses in a narrow alleyway and dodged blocks as she ran. She couldn't enter the house because she saw that it was falling in on itself but she was also aware of her nudity and couldn't go out into the street where she could hear everyone else, including her friend and the visiting pastor, who she definitely did not want to see her naked. So she ran back and forth in the alley trying to avoid the collapsing cement.

But within seconds she realized that now was no time for modesty and she had to get out in the open if she wanted to live. She heard her friends in the street calling her name, worried that she was already lost. With her arms crossed across her chest, she hurried out into the street and stood amidst all of her neighbors all watching their homes sway and break apart. Arriving there she saw that she must not have been the only one in the shower. "Another one of our neighbors was standing there completely naked. He didn't even waste time putting on underwear," she remembered. "So I didn't feel so bad. And no one even noticed right away anyway because everything that was happening around them held their attention."

Eveline wasn't even worried so much about all of the people around her seeing her naked body. Her bigger concern was that she was sure that this was the Second Coming and at any moment the clouds above her were going to open up and Jesus would descend surrounded by His angels. She certainly didn't want to meet her Savior naked.

A second of stillness, then Eveline felt her friend throw a t-shirt over her head. "Now I'm ready," she thought, and she looked up to the heavens welcoming whatever came next. There was noise all around her as people cried and screamed, but she just waited patiently for her Creator to arrive back on the earth. She began to pray out loud, "Oh God all Powerful, forgive me of my sins because I don't even know what I've done but I know the depth of your love. You sent your Son to die for me and you promised that you would come again. Now deliver me from this life." As she prayed she kept her eyes fixed on the sky and lifted her arms out with her palms opened upward. But nothing was happening above her; it seemed that everything that was happening was occurring on the ground around her.

She had heard of earthquakes happening in other places before and began to wonder in her heart if that was what this was. She broke her gaze from above and looked around her to see houses in piles of rubble, people covered in dust and blood, and even her friend's house before her, which she had just escaped, in shambles.

Then she thought about her three sisters across the neighborhood in their own home. As she looked at the house before her which was a one-story house that was strongly built and then thought about her own house where her sisters were which she knew was not as strong and was three stories tall, she broke down herself. "They're dead! They're all dead!" Still in her panties and borrowed shirt, she fell to the ground and wailed, sure that there was no way that they had survived. She joined the masses of mourners wailing over who and what they just lost in an event that none of them understood.

"They're all dead! Oh Jesus! They're dead!"

Then the pastor friend that was there came and knelt beside her. "Have courage, Eveline, they might be just fine. You don't know."

"No! They're gone! They're gone!" She repeated. She was sure in her heart that their old house could not withstand the evil that just passed through the city.

Then the pastor said, "Evelyn, your leg!"

She didn't pay any attention, preoccupied with her sisters, she continued to cry.

"Eveline, you're injured!" He said again.

"Just shut up!" She shouted at him. "My sisters are dead!" But she looked down at her leg to see a large gash across her shin that was bleeding down to her foot. In her frantic exit she hadn't even noticed that a chunk of cement had collided with her leg. The pastor took a handkerchief out of his pocket and wiped off her leg to see where the cut actually was and then tied it around the wound as a bandage.

He put his arm around Eveline and helped her to her feet. "Let's go to the house to see them. I'm sure we'll find them all well."

"No, I can't. I can't." She said and fell to the ground again. "You'd have to get four other men to carry me to the house." She told him, "I can't walk. I can't go see them. They're dead. I know they're dead."

The pastor gave up and left her there to cry.

She stayed there on the ground convinced that even if she escaped the house that she was in, her life was over if her sisters were gone. They were very close. She was the second oldest. Yanick was her big sister, then Souveni was two years younger than Eveline, then Mikerlande was the baby, 18-years-old. They had all come to the city from their rural home in Mizak for a chance at a better education. Eveline knew that at that time in the evening they would have all been at home and she knew that the house was not stable. She lay on the ground and tried to imagine how she would ever move on without them.

As she remained there in her sorrow, the streets around her were infected with a pulsating terror. An anguished sea of people churned, hurrying from place to place and asking about their families. But for Eveline, her world was standing still because she knew where her family was, underneath three stories of cement.

About an hour passed by, but for Eveline it seemed an eternity. Then a voice came from up the street, "Eveline!" It pierced through the crowds and the cries and straight to her ears. It was Mikerlande! Eveline looked up and peered through the bodies to see all three of her sisters running towards her. She jumped up just as they got to her and the four of them embraced rejoicing in sounds that only the ears of angels could understand.

"I thought you were all dead." Eveline told them.

"We're all fine. We knew you would be fine too, but we had to come find you." Yanick said.

Eveline felt her world begin to turn again. Her tears stopped flowing and she knew that now she was going to be okay. Her sisters told her that they were going to return to their home, even though it too was destroyed. They wanted to be there in case their mother came looking for them. Eveline decided to stay where she was with her friend. Now that she knew her sisters were okay, she knew she would be okay too.

That night they all met up again, however, as they congregated with hundreds of others at a soccer field to sleep in the open. The four Louis sisters, the friend, the pastor, and the entire community from that area of the city all slept as far away from any cement as they could. With the earth still shaking on and off, no one knew what might fall from above next, sending them to sleep in the open.

In the coming days they all started to build shelters on that soccer field with tarps, and sheets, and scrap metal, and whatever else they could find, and they stayed in those shelters for weeks to come. In those weeks Eveline became more and more discouraged with every day that passed. She knew that she had survived something that many did not, but she felt that this was certainly no way to live. They had lost all possessions that they had in the collapse of their own house and were now living like animals in refugee camps just yards away from where they used to enjoy a comfortable existence. Her leg was not healing well and she was beginning to miss school. She told her sisters that they had to do something because they couldn't stay like this forever.

About a month after the quake they began looking for another place to rent in the city, but tin roofed homes had become far too expensive. Souveni had been talking about returning to Mizak, where at least their father had a good home, and they would be able to find food to eat. Eventually all the sisters agreed that they had no other choice and they decided to head back out into the countryside.

They boarded a tap-tap at Kafou to take them as far as Jacmel. Eveline sat down in her favorite position at the very back of the bench where you get the most air. As other passengers got on the truck, one young man, about Eveline's age, got on and told Eveline to scoot over so he could sit where she was. Eveline was still not in a very good mood about having to leave Port-au-Prince and was not hopeful about the future, so she didn't respond kindly to the man trying to push her around. "Just step past me!" She told him bluntly. But then she took a moment to reflect and felt like maybe God was telling her to give up her spot for some reason and she scooted over to let the man sit down, but she kept the scowl on her face.

When he sat down he asked her why she was so grumpy. "What business is it of yours?" She snapped at him. But then she looked towards the front at Souveni and Mikerlande who were both giving her looks that suggested she needed to lighten up. "I'm sorry," she said,

"I'm still just a little bit worked up about everything that I've been through with the earthquake."

"That's okay. We all are." He told her. "Where are you from?" He asked.

"Mizak, LaVallee of Jacmel." Eveline responded.

He didn't believe her. He thought that all people from Jacmel were easy-going and friendly. Eveline hadn't convinced him that she was one of them.

"No really, we're actually headed back there right now. Those are my three sisters there," she said, and pointed to them up front. "We've lived in the city for three years, but since the earthquake, we've decided to return to Mizak." She went on to tell him how they had gotten to that point and what she had experienced on the 12th.

The man, then, of course began to tell his story, the story that all Haitians had perfected and told over and over by that point. But Eveline was not ready for his.

This man was at work, on the third floor, the top floor of his building, when the goudougoudou struck. His building immediately began to collapse and he fell to the floor and crouched underneath the iron chair that he was sitting in as the concrete fell down around him. The chair protected him from being smothered underneath the fallen structure and created a small pocket of space for him to survive. But when the earth stopped trembling he was trapped inside surrounded by cement.

He couldn't see anything but blackness all around him. He sent his hands to the left and to the right and felt cement within arm's reach each direction. He shifted his body into the small space that he felt on both sides so that he was now laying on his back with his legs still pulled up against his stomach. And there he stayed, in the fetal position, still breathing, but unable to move, unable to escape.

He had no clue what had just happened, and there was nothing he could do to find out. He just laid there. And laid there. And laid there. In the darkness and stillness he heard the sounds of others below and around him trapped in the same building yelling desperately hoping to be saved.

"As time went on their cries became less and less distinguishable." He told Eveline. "Soon I couldn't even make out the words that they were crying and it just started to sound like thousands of bees buzzing underneath the cement that I was laying on."

He laid there trapped and faded in and out of consciousness with only the buzzing to listen to and his own confused thoughts to occupy his mind, his sanity began to fade as well. Time was passing but he had no idea how much. Minutes. Hours. Days, perhaps. He laid there. He grew hungry and thirsty and his body was filled with pain but as his mental state grew weaker and weaker he began to turn numb physically as well. He could tell that he wasn't dead, yet, but knew that it was just a matter of time.

Every so often he could feel the earth shift again, each time shaking more dust and debris onto him in his tiny life hole.

The buzzing grew quieter and quieter.

Then, all at once, another tremor disrupted the stillness, this one bigger than the others before it, and shook more morsels of cement upon the man's body. He closed his eyes to shield from the dust and kept them closed for a couple minutes while he still felt the debris in the air around him. Then, when he slowly opened them, he was startled to see something that he hadn't seen since the first quake had trapped him there... light.

Convinced that his time had come and he was finally headed towards the bright light of Heaven, he took a deep breath expecting to find peace. But when he inhaled, he coughed, his lungs filling with dust. "If this is heaven," he thought, "why is the air still so dirty?"

He realized that he was still alive and the light shining through the cement into where he was lying was coming from outside. He squinted through the light reflecting off of the particles filling the air to try to understand where exactly the opening was. This last tremor had shaken loose the chunks of cement providing a possible escape. He started crawling slowly over the cement around him towards the light. As he crawled he still heard the buzzing under him, but he left it behind now with the hope that he was going to survive.

He reached the opening and squeezed through the crevice that had appeared. "It was small and I scrapped up my back as I pulled myself through," he said and then pulled up his shirt to show Eveline the marks that were still visible on his back.

Once out, he simply collapsed on top of the rubble, stretched out his legs, and took a few moments to look at the world around him and convince himself that he was going to be okay. He knew that under the cement that he was lying on there were still people dying, but he was alive. He was alive.

As he laid there, someone walking by noticed him and shouted, "This man's alive!" The woman ran up to him and said, "Are you okay?" He just groaned, unable to speak through the hunger and thirst. "Get this man some water!" She yelled out into the street. Soon another man came up with a bottle of water and he poured it over his face and then gave him a drink. He swallowed and then took the bottle with his own hand and drank the rest.

The man and woman helped him to his feet, and to his surprise, he could stand. He stood and with the two strangers' help, he began to walk over the rubble and out into the street. The woman found a chair for him to sit on and the man found a package of cookies to give him to eat and another bottle of water. After that he began to feel his strength return, but he sat there for a couple hours longer to let reality sink into his head.

The woman sat there and talked to him and that is when he first heard that it was an earthquake. "What day is today?" he asked her.

It had been four days since the first quake struck that he had been trapped inside of the building that he had just escaped. January 16th, 2010. The woman continued to explain to him what the last four days had been like and how the quake had devastated not only Port-au-

Prince but a large area of the country. Until he talked to her, he had no idea that anything had happened beyond his building.

Eveline listened to the man's story in the back of the tap-tap and recalls later, "It was like this man sitting next to me wasn't even there anymore, but it was Jesus Christ speaking through him. That is the only way to explain it. His life had been so torn apart that if he was able to sit there next to me and speak about any of it, it was God Almighty who was doing the talking."

But his story wasn't over yet. After talking to the woman and beginning to regain his state of mind, he realized that he had to go to his family. They were surely mourning his death and he had to go find them so that they would know he was alive.

He then rose to his feet and found that he had the strength from somewhere to hurry off in the direction of his house. He went through the city past flattened buildings, bodies in the streets, and crowds of people in open fields, but paid all of that little mind because he was focused on his destination.

When he arrived at his address, he found his home in a pile of dust. In that moment his spirit decomposed and he lost the strength to stand. Melting to the ground he cried out for his family that had surely died there in the home. He could smell the death in the air coming from all around him, including right before him where his family's home used to be. He laid there crying for hours until he had no tears left inside him. "Why would I have been saved if I was just to find my family eliminated like this?" He wondered. He wished in that moment that the rubble had never opened up to let him escape. He would have rather suffocated there with the rest of the buzzing bees.

He thought that if his family was gone, he must go find some of his friends to find consolation in his grief. He remembered that four days ago, when he got off of work he had a wedding to go to for one of his good friends. He went off towards the nearby church where the wedding was to be held. As he approached the church he found it in a pile of rubble as well. He also smelled the same odor of death and knew that there were surely bodies under that rubble as well. But at this time he didn't cry. He had no emotions left at all. His soul had abandoned him. He was simply a body walking through the streets to find more and more reasons to give up on life.

He found a neighbor near the church who confirmed what he feared, on the 12th the church collapsed on the entire wedding party and the congregation of people gathered to celebrate, just as the bride was walking down the aisle. The only person who did not die in the collapse was the groom who was arriving late and was in the street in front of the church right when the earth started shaking. He stood there and watched his true love, and everyone close to him, die in an instant. He did not survive though, as he saw this happen before him, he fell into a seizure right there in the street and died from the trauma.

Then, four days later, another man stood there realizing that he had lost everyone that meant anything to him too. But he did not seize. He was dead inside already.

Now, a month later, that same man, still hadn't rediscovered life as he sat next to Eveline Louis on the tap-tap and recounted his experience. He had come from a shack that he had constructed in one of the local refugee camps where he now existed by himself but he didn't know where he was going. He felt his life had nowhere to go.

Even if he had no destination on that tap-tap, Eveline knew why he was there. Fate had put him there next to her as a wake-up call. "It was after talking to that man that I quit feeling sorry for myself and started being thankful for what I had. I saw that no matter how bad things may seem sometimes, there is always somebody worse off."

After telling his story, the man told Evelyn good-bye and got off at the next stop. "I never even thought to ask his name or get a phone number. I was so stunned by what he had been through. He had absolutely no one left in this world. I should have thought to at least get a phone number so that I could be someone for him. He needed a friend, and I needed a reality check." But she wasn't able to become his friend. She watched him walk away as the truck moved forward.

She turned to look at her sisters in the front through tears in her eyes and smiled. She got up and went to sit next to Yanick and reached across the aisle to hold Mikerlande's hand. She laid her head on Yanick's shoulder and said a silent and simple prayer to God, "Lord, forgive me. Forgive me and walk with this man who needs somebody by his side right now. I may not be able to help him, Lord, but you can be there for him. I thank you for my life. It is in your hands. Thank you.

ARTWORK BY RONALD MARDI

SOMETHING STRANGE IN THE AIR

No one could have expected or prepared for what upturned their lives that day. Although there were some popular pastors in the country who had predicted the event beforehand, proclaiming that earthquakes would devastate the land in the beginning of the year. They had analyzed scripture and warned the public of what they believed would be tragic times. But when the claims were first made, no one really believed these fundamentalists raving in the streets. As superstitious as Haitians may be even most of them weren't buying this. But even those few who did believe the future telling pastors could never have been ready for what occurred on the 12th.

It was several days after the quake when Julie brought a small sheet of paper out of the house to show me as I was sitting out front. It was a sheet of paper with a message by one of these pastors warning of an impending disaster. She had gotten it back in October 2009. It was eerie reading how accurate his words were. He talked about the hurricanes and other disasters that had shocked Haiti and then compared them with passages from the Bible that suggested that early in the year 2010 a devastating earthquake unlike anything the world has ever seen would wreak havoc on this country.

These warnings on little sheets of paper had spread all over the country the previous fall. I had received one too, but I discarded and disregarded mine right away. I even remember joking with Papi and Berthony about how crazy the pastors were to think that they could predict such a thing. Julie said she didn't know why she kept hers, she didn't believe it when she first received it either, but there it was, days after the quake, proving that someone had a feeling about this long before it ever happened.

Even on that day though, January 12th, there was something strange in the air from the beginning, especially in Port-au-Prince. Everyone in the city recalls an uneasy feeling that was floating in the air ever since they woke up that morning. Gina noticed that there were no taxis in service as she left to go to work at the preschool where she taught. After trying to find a ride for over an hour, she gave up and went home deciding that there must be a reason she wasn't supposed to go to work that day. At the end of the day she found out that her school building had collapsed. A tap-tap driver that I know well, says that he decided not to go out driving that day because he sensed something dangerous looming in the streets also. Others commented on how confused they were to find that very few businesses were functioning that day. It was much more difficult than usual just to find a place to buy some sugar. It was clear that something wasn't right. The spirit of the city was anticipating something out of the ordinary, but no one had any idea what was coming their way at 4:53 that afternoon.

For Eveline Louis' sister, Souveni, she knew as soon as she woke up that she couldn't go to school. She couldn't explain why. She wasn't sick. She didn't have any other appointments. And the weather was just fine. But the atmosphere was turbulent and she was unwilling to expose herself to whatever evil might be brewing beyond what she could see with her eyes. Souveni told her mother, Simone, this. Simone, seeing how much distress her daughter was in, agreed that she could stay home from school and told her to go to her sister's house in Kafou and wait for her there. She was going to go ahead and see if she could go out in the city and make any sales as usual, but, if business was not good, she told her daughter she would join her in Kafou after work. Souveni tried to convince her not to go, but just go straight to Kafou with her for the day instead. Simone knew, however, that she could not sacrifice a single day's work in order to provide for her daughters.

Simone Durée sold staples such as rice, corn, and beans, in bulk in a small depot in the city with a couple other women. She went to work that day, against her daughter's advice, thinking that she needed to make a little money, but from the start it seemed that Souveni's premonitions may have been substantial. The flow of the city was stagnant. No one was out to purchase and business was discouraging. Simone sat with her business partners for hours that morning without making any sales. After a while one of them decided not to waste her time anymore and left to go home. Simone and the other decided to stay a little longer and see if they couldn't make at least one sale before giving up on the day.

Finally one woman came by and ordered five small barrels of corn. The partner went inside to prepare the woman's order while Simone collected the woman's money. Five barrels was a rather large purchase, so Simone invited her inside rather than having her expose the handful of cash in the open street. Once the customer had paid, she turned to start taking her barrels outside to the truck that was waiting and Simone took her money and tied it in a small cloth pouch tucked inside her skirt. It was at that moment that Simone felt a rumbling and thought that one of the large road construction vehicles must have been passing by. Then the house began to tremble and four bags of rice fell to the ground and spilled onto the feet of the two women.

Simone grabbed her business partner in her arms and held her. "Let's go die outside!" She yelled and they began running towards the door. As they stepped towards the door they slipped on the rice and fell to the floor. "Anmwey!" They both began to scream and covered their heads with their hands.

A moment later the ground stilled and they both jumped up and ran outside into the open yard next to their building. Neither of them understood what was going on. They looked around and didn't even see the woman who had just bought the corn. All they saw were people running and crying out. They saw a chaos that could not be understood.

Simone thought about her daughters and remembered what Souveni had sensed that morning. She told her partner to be careful and she began walking towards Kafou to be with her girls. *Step. Step.* As she walked, it was difficult for her to even pick out the details of what she saw. She didn't see bodies, or broken buildings, or cracks in the cement, or dust in the air at first. All that she saw was pandemonium, an overwhelming atmosphere of incomprehensible confusion, but she pressed on through the confusion with a single goal in mind, to see her daughters.

When the details started to come into focus and she noticed bodies and realized that people had died in whatever it was that just passed by and spilled her rice, she got a knot in her stomach. If all of these people had died, what about her four girls? She began to walk faster. *Step, step, step.* Then she stopped again. She closed her eyes, took a deep breath, and was filled with a sense of peace again. She knew in her heart her children were okay. She ignored the disorder around her and continued to walk.

She walked by the St. Joseph Church and saw that the steeple had fallen and walls had broken. She had always loved walking by this church on her way home from work and couldn't believe that its beauty had been destroyed so quickly. She paused for a moment to look at the structure. She had walked by victims with their stomachs ripped open and their entrails spilled on the ground. She had walked by the incinerated gas pump and all of its charred victims. She had walked by people with limbs crushed and heads severed and flesh stripped off the bone, but none of that fazed her. Yet seeing the steeple of this church diminished to rubble gripped her heart and she allowed herself to ask for reasons.

She heard people in the streets crying out to God, but she couldn't believe he was responsible. She had just seen that extraordinary structure that was built for his glory crushed and eliminated. But she also could see that no force of man could cause such extreme mayhem. She contemplated it all in her mind but she didn't have answers to any of her questions. What she did have was a determination fixed on finding her daughters amidst it all. She kept walking. *Step. Step. Step.*

When Simone arrived at Kafou and approached the location of her daughters' home she saw everyone along the way crying and calling out the names of those that they had lost. Many homes in the neighborhood were destroyed, but she kept the hope in her heart that her girls were okay. When she made it to the house she saw the roof of the three story building flat on the ground and knew that if anyone was inside there was no way that they survived. But something quiet inside her still nudged her towards belief that her babies were okay.

She asked the neighbors if they had seen the girls or knew if they were alright. But Simone couldn't get a clear response from anyone because they were all consumed by their own grief. No one knew where her daughters were and she seemed to be the only one choosing hope. She looked back at the decimated home and doubt began to creep in. Maybe she was just naive. Maybe she needed to accept reality. Her body slowly melted to the ground and she began to cry, not in the way everyone around her was crying with wailing and convulsions, but with a small, subtle acceptance of her loss, she cried.

It wasn't long, however, that she cried there on the ground until she heard a voice from up the street, "Mama!" It was the same voice that Eveline had heard moments before, Mickerlande. "Mama, get up off the ground! Mama! We're okay!" She cried.

All three sisters then ran and picked Simone up off the ground and embraced her in their arms. "I knew you were okay. I knew I couldn't lose you." Simone told them. "The neighbors made me lose hope, but in my heart I knew you were there."

"We're here Mama," Yanick said, "And Eveline's fine too."

"Praise Jesus, the Eternal!" Simone cried. "Praise God!"

When they got done rejoicing together, they found a spot nearby to sit down and rest. Simone was exhausted after having walked across town trying to maintain an impossible hope the whole time.

As the four of them sat there and talked the girls asked their mother if she knew anything about her younger sister, their Aunt Myceline. Myceline had been taking classes at a local vocational school where she would have been at the time of the quake. The girls had heard people say that the school was destroyed but they didn't know anything about their aunt. Simone felt rested up by that time and decided to go look for her sister at the school which wasn't too far from the girl's place in Kafou.

It was the middle of the night by that time so Simone took a flashlight out of her purse which was still in her hand since she had left her business that afternoon and went to the school. Once she got there she saw the building just as her daughters had said, completely laid to ruin. There was a small group of people sitting nearby the crumpled building covered in dust that seemed to be survivors from the school. Simone went and talked to them and asked if they knew her sister, Myceline Duree.

One young woman did know Myceline and said that she was in the same class as her when the ground began quaking, but since she made it out herself, she hadn't seen Myceline. The woman stood up and took Simone to show her the place where their classroom was. "There," she said and pointed to a pile of cement wreckage. "Not many students made it out in time," she explained to Simone.

But Simone chose to continue holding on to hope, seeing how it had worked out before. She stood there right next to the pile of concrete talking to the woman, "Myceline will be alright. Myceline will be alright." She said partly to herself, partly to the sister's classmate, and partly to the heavens. Then they paused in talking for a moment for Simone to shine her light over the rubble to see if it was really worth the hope.

As she shone her light she heard someone faintly call her name, "Simone!" She looked around to see if someone behind her had seen her but saw no one. "Simone!" She heard again.

Maybe she was just imagining things, the voice being just a fabrication of her hope. She asked the woman next to her if she heard it too. "Yes, shhhhh. Listen." She told her.

"Simone! Is that you?"

Simone shone her light on the collapsed building in front of her again. The voice was coming from under the cement!

"Myceline!" Simone cried out. "Myceline! Is it really you?" The voice was weak but she recognized it as her sister's. "Myceline! Are you alright?" She got closer to the cement where she thought she heard the voice and shined her light in all the cracks and the spaces. She saw arms and other limbs and couldn't tell if they belonged to bodies alive or dead. "Myceline, keep talking!"

"Simone! I'm here!"

Myceline had been trapped under the rubble ever since the quake caused her school to fall on top of her but was not injured. She laid there in the darkness for hours with nowhere to go. She could see nothing and there was cement all around her, so although she was unscathed and free inside, she could find no way out. After many hours she gave up and began to confess her sins, sure that she was going to die. As she was praying she felt a force telling her stop. Then she heard a voice, "Myceline is going to be alright." At first she thought it was God speaking to her telling her that he would take care of her. But then she heard it again, "Myceline is going to be alright."

That's when she realized that it wasn't God's voice at all. It was her sister Simone's.

That's when she cried out and her sister heard her underneath the concrete. When Simone began shining her light into the cracks, Myceline noticed it and was able to see a space before her that looked large enough to crawl through. "Simone! I'm here! Hold the light there!" She called out.

The light stopped and Simone yelled into the rubble, "Myceline, are you okay?"

Myceline began to crawl toward the light. As she did she heard other voices under and around her. "No! Don't step there!" "You're going to kill me! Don't move!" As she crawled other chunks of cement shifted below her and she wasn't sure of the consequences for the others trapped under the rubble. She heard them scream but she knew this was her only chance to make it out and she kept crawling towards her sister's flashlight. She made it to the opening and reached her hand out.

"Simone! It's me!" Simone grabbed her sister's hand and the classmate reached in to take her shoulder so they could pull her out.

"I thought I was dead." Myceline told her sister. "I thought there was no way out until I heard your voice."

Now with her sister in her arms, Simone had all the reasons that she needed to rejoice and thank God that her hope was not in vain. She had listened to the quiet tugging at her soul and that hope had brought her through. It may even be what saved her sister and that strength is what kept her daughters believing in life as well. Now they just had to find a way to hold onto that same hope through tomorrow and the days to come.

ARTWORK BY ALEXANDRA AMAZAN

PIECING LIFE TOGETHER

Through the first weeks I still teetered on the side of doubt when it came to God, but on the second Sunday after the quake I decided to give God a chance, and I went to church. When I arrived it was clear that I wasn't the only one wanting to talk to God. The church was fuller than I had ever seen it. I have to admit that I questioned people's intentions for being there. I wondered how many of them actually needed the praise and prayer with fellow believers and how many of them were there because they'd suffered damage to their homes and knew about the international connections of the church and hoped that their attendance would increase their chances of receiving aid for their homes. I'd seen that effect at this and other churches before when hardship would strike.

Whatever the case, they were all there, and they all had something to say. In the musical portion of the service the church always invites anyone who wants to come to the front to share a song or just their thoughts or prayer requests. This Sunday that portion lasted three times longer than usual with everyone wanting to share. Some just got up and told everybody what they should be thinking at a time like this. Others just sang their song and asked for prayers because they have so many problems. The rest just waved their hands in the air and shouted praises to the Lord.

I attempted to understand that everyone was searching, and no one had answers, including myself, but the questions inside of me were too unrelenting to listen to more fluff. I had reached my limit of that stuff because after so much it all quickly began sounding the same. The suffering became so generalized that those praises and prayer requests begin to sound like a skipping CD.

In his 1944 novel, The Masters of the Dew, Haitian writer, Jacques Roumain, opens the book with a character named Bienamie reflecting upon his wife's prayers with the following thoughts:

> But so many poor creatures call continually upon the Lord that it makes a big bothersome noise. When the Lord hears it, he yells, "What the hell's all that?" and stops up his ears. Yes, he does, leaving man to shift for himself.

As I sat there in church, I could imagine the Lord stopping up his ears and muttering to the angels about all the racket. So I didn't stay out in the service long but went in the back room and talked with Serge, one of my LMI co-founders. He agreed with me that it was all too much. It was clear that after almost two weeks people were still lost in the moment of the quake. They perhaps saw no other options but to dwell in the confusion. I sat there with Serge thinking about how it all was only going to make them crazier. Serge agreed with me that although we by no means should pretend like the earthquake didn't happen, we had to find a better way to deal with its reality. We had to find a way to begin, however so slowly it may be, to move on. We needed to deal with it in ways that were deeper and more effective at helping us begin to take steps towards recovery.

Later in his book, Roumain writes:

> *What good are prayers and orations when comes this last hour that the Book talks about: when the moon goes out and the stars go out and the wax of the clouds masks the sun. When the courageous Negro says, "I am tired," and the Negress stops grinding the corn because she is tired. When there is a bird in the woods laughing like a rusty rattle and those who sing are sitting in a circle without a word and without a sound and those who cry run around Main Street and cry, "Help me, help me! because today we bury our man and he is going to the graveyard, to his tomb, to dust.*

We had reached that hour when everyone was still crying for those who the Grinder had sent to their tombs and prayers could do no good.

These prayers consisted of the same empty phrases repeated over and over that just pitter-patter on the surface without ever penetrating the spirit. Just a bunch of words filled with helium floating away to a place where the petitioners hope some magic dwells. I had begun to fear that maybe it was just my own soul that had become impenetrable, but I continued to search along with everyone else, if not for answers to what passed, at least for reason in the present moments. Whatever I may have told myself I was craving, it was clear that it wouldn't be found in any church.

Serge was on the same page as me though. He agreed that the cookie cutter petitions to God that were heard in the church were not going to help the people find any resolution to their problems whether they be physical, emotional, or spiritual. There had to be a better way. There was beauty within each other's stories, no matter how traumatic they may be, that deserved to be shared and expressed.

It was also that morning that I decided that I personally needed to start piecing life back together. I wasn't going to dwell anymore like those people that I saw in church.

That's why I decided that night that I was going to sleep back in the guest house where I had been living. Sure, there were still occasional light aftershocks, but nothing strong enough to damage the house again, so I was going to face the fear and sleep back inside again. I was able to persuade Berthony and Papi to join me inside again, but Sony decided he was going to stick to the grass in front of Astrel's house a little longer. The three of us, however, resolved to sleep back in our beds, a symbolic effort to move forward.

It took a few seconds to realize that it wasn't just another nightmare, but that the earth was actually shaking again. Strongly. Before I could even jump up, Berthony ran by the couch where I was sleeping and grabbed me and pushed me outside. I heard something behind us fall off the shelf and break. The movement didn't stop until we were out in the open. It wasn't near as bad as the original quake, but definitely the strongest tremor that we had had since. It was strong enough to wake Berthony and I up and send us running for safety away from the already cracked walls. Once calmness returned Bethony looked at me and said, "You're barefoot!"

"You think I was going to take the time to put on sandals?" I said.

We didn't see Papi. Apparently we had forgotten about any sort of strength in numbers when we felt the world tremble again, and all hurried to save ourselves. We heard Papi yell from inside, "Thanks a lot for leaving me in here to die alone, guys!" He tried to escape out of the window in his room but got blocked by the gutter outside, so he just surrendered himself to fate inside. Fate favored him and nothing happened.

Berthony and I walked back in and shined my flashlight to see my bottle of cologne broken on the floor along with a couple other things that were on the shelf, deodorant, a toothbrush, and some batteries. We laid back down, this time all three on the one queen sized bed that we had in the house, but none of us slept the rest of the night.

The next morning we heard the news, this tremor was a 6.1 intensity and caused more devastation in the already hardest hit areas. More buildings collapsed. More lives lost. It toppled my newly gained confidence once again too. That night we decided to return to Astrel's yard and sleep under the stars, which I knew would be falling once more.

As we walked back to the grass patch under the almond tree with our sheets and pillows under our arms once more, the structure that Astrel's family had fashioned together where we had been sleeping spoke to me in a way that started to make sense. The majority of it was made from what the Haitians call "convergence" sheets. These sheets are made by piecing together different large scraps of fabric, usually in drab colors of navy, black, and gray, that come from old pairs of pants or church shirts that have gotten too small for the owner or worn out and unwearable. Craftsmen take these items of clothing, cut them at the seams and sew them back together in large square sections to construct the convergence sheets. And it was these sheets that thousands of families all over the country had made tents out of in the last week and a half to live under. The sheets themselves seemed to reflect the lives that the Haitian people were living at that time.

I had seen these primitive quilts around ever since I came to Haiti, but never thought much about them. Then after the quake they popped up all over the place as people used them to shelter their lives. This was before the inundation of bright blue tarps from aid agencies made everyone's pathetic tents at least waterproof. Everyone just threw up walls of their old pants sewn together. And that worked. I lived in a shelter like this for two weeks after the quake there in front of Astrel's house and it was there that I spent some of the most significant moments of my life.

The poignancy of these sheets described something to me that no prayer could at that time of survival. I felt my life and Haitian's lives in general were just like those sheets, pieces of random discarded scraps thrown together into something sort of complete in an attempt to justify existence. The sheets themselves looked like something a hobo in a Mark Twain novel would use to cover himself at night. And here, the entire population had become wanderers, nomads in their own country, trying to find security in whatever leftover remnants of life they could scavenge up.

These sheets had become Haitian's homes. But if you walked up to one of these homes the convergence walls themselves would say to you, "The lives of the people living here are incomplete. Some pieces of the puzzle are missing. But we're doing the best we can."

Sure, an aid agency can come donate a bright blue tarp to one of these families and it may start to say "in one piece" but it's still not complete. It's still a sad joke of an existence sheltered by some power from without. The lives inside may be dry but they are not yet whole. The glossy plastic just camouflages the emotional walls still crumbling and laying scattered on the unsteady earth. Those were the pieces that needed to be put back together.

These emotional pieces were the ones that could not be put back together by any team of swoopers. They were the ones that could not be shown by any news camera or seen on any internet site. Buildings were not the only things that were crushed on January 12th. Dignity, confidence, faith, reason and hope. These are the things that one cannot rebuild. They cannot be replaced by a tarp with an organization's name on it.

Even though I was going to sleep outside on Astrel's grass for a few more days, I decided that I had to consciously begin taking action to put some of my own pieces back together. I knew where I had to start. My house was still sitting there as a sad daily reminder of what happened. About that time there was a team of American doctors who did swoop through Mizak and when one of them saw my house he fittingly described it as looking like a house painted by Salvador Dali. It was still visibly a house, but not a normal one. One that exists in some surreal world where nothing is solid, where nothing is as it seems. It's not like the houses in Port-au-Prince or Jacmel that look more like they came out of a Jackson Pollack or Pablo Picasso painting not resembling the original structure at all, where everything has become completely abstract and you have to use a lot of imagination to even believe that they are meant to represent houses.

I've always been a fan of Dali, but I would never move into any house found in one of his paintings. I had decided it was time to tear it apart the rest of the way and start over. Having it there reminding me of what it almost could have been was really more discouraging than if it had been obliterated into a pile of unidentifiable dust. Every time I walked by it I would still pick up another rock to hurl at the walls that continued to mock me. That wasn't helping me put any pieces back together. So I called up my construction workers and the next day they got right to work beginning to break down the structure.

The destruction process of a work of art can be very cathartic once you accept its necessity and begin to see what waits on the other side. Re-creation. In the case of my house I found it very therapeutic to watch the workers eliminate what was there. It was something real beginning to happen. It was movement. It was something that I was in control of. Though I may not have been the one actually doing the breaking down, it was my decision.

I felt like I had passed an incredible hurdle with this, however, the same mouths that broke the house in the first place were still searching for reasons to criticize. The very fact that I was not in there breaking down the remainder of the house with my own hands was apparently unacceptable to some. These mouths were saying that if I was going to break the house down, why didn't my roommates and I do it ourselves. After all, anyone can swing a sledgehammer and toss chunks of cement into piles. The insinuation, once again, feeling like we weren't doing anything productive anyways, at least this would give us something to do.

The only respectable forms of helping at that point seemed to be pulling bodies out of the debris, or volunteering at the hospital, or handing out water at the airport, but not sharing stories with the local victims and writing down thoughts and feelings. If I was doing those other things then no one would think I had time to swing a sledgehammer. I wasn't sure why everyone back home was so desperate for evidence of me being active. They seemed to be waiting for some photos of me sweating and some stories of me saving to show everyone back home.

Those who know me well know that I'm one of those people who, when told that I shouldn't do something, or even more, that I can't do something, that will only inspire me to work even harder to do it. The criticisms from the States fueled me.

I felt a need to prove to people that if they wanted to make decisions about what should be done here then they could go ahead and devote their entire lives to this place and the people here. They could make the sacrifices that I'd made. They could learn the language and build a solid reputation in the community. They could come build a house to live in just to see it destroyed. If they wanted to make the decisions then they had to make the devotion. They could paint me as the martyr, they could paint me as the victim, but pressuring me to be a hero through their foreign interpretations of what needed to be done was not helping. I adopted this attitude to propel me forward and prevent the negative words from weighing down on me. It was this attitude that pushed me through any fear that remained.

The mouths in Haiti continued to make their noise as well saying that it was too early to begin working on the house again. The aftershocks were still occurring. Only a crazy person would think he could start building again. No one even knew when the aftershocks would stop completely. Some were saying they would continue for months to come. And if I was planning on rebuilding it with a cement roof again, then I must have been completely nuts! I must have been just asking to be crushed by cement. Sure it was a phenomenal view on top of the roof, but it wasn't worth dying for!

I heard everything they said, but I wasn't going to waste my time with fear of the unknown any more. I was going to start stitching the pieces of my convergence sheet back together. I was reclaiming control.

Because out of all of the things that the Grinder took away from us, that was the one thing that seemed to be slipping away more and more each day but no one seemed interested in helping the victims get it back. Control. Homes, schools, hospitals, clinics, businesses, work, money, food, stability, progress, dignity, activity, celebrations, mothers, fathers, sons, daughters, friends... Some of these things could be rebuilt, regained, or given back in time. Others were lost forever.

Everyone in the country appreciated the food, and the tents, and the medicine, but what they would have really liked at that point was to feel like they held control in their blistered hands once more. They had lost control of their lives. They had lost control of their destinies. They had lost control of their country. Handouts couldn't do anything to remedy that. Charity couldn't give them back the control that had been stolen from them. And even if no foreign nations were officially occupying Haiti, we all knew that they really might as well have been. Haitians had been rendered powerless, helpless, left without options. They had lost control over what tomorrow might look like.

They needed some force to start building them back up, restoring their confidence and giving them a shove back in a forward moving direction where they didn't have to just sit around waiting for someone else to save them. Then they could say "This is what we're going to do for ourselves and this is how we're going to do it because this is what our country needs."

This was the country's only chance to assume an ownership for their country that they've never had the chance to really claim. There's always been some other foreign influence messing things up for them. And even in the aftermath, many continued to mess things up. But it was clear that the only way to put the country back together was with Haitian hands. Slowly control would force itself to be rediscovered.

ARTWORK BY RONALD MARDI

ALPHABET SOUP

There are certain countries that instill in their citizens a belief that, when they see a messy situation, their nationality has bought them the right to go get involved in making it messier. The single scariest thing in these situations is a bunch of people with good hearts wanting to help but absolutely no cultural knowledge or experience. Good intentions without an understanding of shared humanity are the cause of so many millions and even billions of dollars in aid going to waste as the victims' dignity gets trampled along the way. The swoopers come in, spend a week, they sweat and they serve doing jobs that the Haitians could have done, then they take their photos back home to show everyone that donated how much "help" they provided. But the Haitians' lives remain the same.

As they leave, those of us who live here frequently find ourselves shaking our heads and telling our Haitian friends, "Well their hearts were in the right place," in an attempt to justify their ignorance and encourage the Haitians not to judge our whole country based on their misguided actions. We say their hearts were in the right place because we're ashamed to admit that their minds are still unknowingly lost in ethnocentric perceptions of poverty.

The religious ones come in on a pretext of "helping the least of these" as if their intention is to degrade those who are implied to be less than them. Some higher power that allegedly equals love deemed these people "greater than" somewhere along the way and now whether it is their own savior complexes, or guilt, that drives them they come with a disconnected sense of pity that leaves no lasting impression on Haiti or its people. The non-religious ones come to prove that you don't have to be religious to help the poor dirty brown folks. They come for the cheap sweet rum, the cheap sweet sex, or the cheap sweet beaches. They come because they're disenchanted with life where they come from and end up here searching for some sort of meaning. The Haitians involuntarily become the extras in the movies that these people are writing in their minds about themselves.

I write this with the full knowledge that most people would put me into one of these categories. As many times as people both Haitian and non, say that I am indeed Haitian, I am not. I am still that Iowan farm boy that came to this country with preconceived notions of the people who were here and how I was intending to help them. Hopefully I've changed since then but no matter how much I adapt to the culture, my skin color, my accent, and my belief systems that still influence my thinking prevent me from ever fully dissolving into the culture. It's a necessary reconciliation we all must confront when doing "this type of work". Most people when traveling into an environment like this, where the people are materially poorer and the country lacks in physical development, they come in with a mindset of "helping" "service" "ministry" "mission" "aid" and all of these mindsets draw unnecessary lines between "us" and "them". The ones providing the service and the ones being served are clearly not in the same category. There are always "those less fortunate" and those with "something to offer".

Concerning oneself with mission, or social justice, or aid or relief, or doing unto the least of these, distracts from the simple sacredness of living life with other humans. Even if those other humans have had much different opportunities from birth and face much different struggles day to day we still must recognize the splendid truth that stitches us together and makes souls converge. And through that recognition we see how helping others is no longer a virtue to strive for, or a marketing tool for a website, but is simply something that happens in the process of living.

This is the reconciliation that I discovered myself in. As an artist this meant that my artwork began taking on a much different route than most as we all search for beauty to communicate and a space to communicate it in. My help became my art as my art has always been my life.

Because of this I resisted the seemingly inevitable creation of another organization to carry out this work. It killed me that I had to invent one more acronym to add to the alphabet soup. If there was a way for human beings to accompany fellow human beings in different countries as they search for the beauty in life without having to fill out paperwork for the IRS and the Haitian Minister of Social Affairs and writing mission statements and visions and objectives and all of that, then that was what I wanted to do. But, unfortunately, the artwork that I wanted to do in collaboration with my Haitian neighbors required significant funds, and finding those funds required the paperwork and organizational hoopla. So I followed through and filled out the papers adding Living Media International to the mix.

Nonetheless, I still resisted all of the NGO formulas as much as possible and encouraged my cofounders and early collaborators to do the same. After the earthquake, especially, the necessity to change the mindset became much clearer as all of those lines separating peoples fell into the earth and disappeared. When we laid with each other on the ground singing and praying for survival, fearing the aftershocks, there was no "me" or "you". There was just "us". That sacred connection within this unity revealed the foundation for our organization to be built upon. It is not about any one group of people ministering to any one other group of people. It is simply about human beings collaborating together to make life more beautiful. Across borders and beyond cultural differences, anyone involved in this work becomes an artist searching for the beauty in life and developing new ways to express that beauty to those who don't yet recognize it.

It was after the earthquake that the work I wanted to do became even more important, but at the same time, it was then, more than ever, that I was ashamed to add one more organization to the mix. It was in the epoch of the Grinder that the alphabet soup got even thicker and more offensive to taste. Famed photojournalist, James Nachtwey, came into the country after the quake and summed up what he saw this way:

> *The earth shrugged, Haiti collapsed and the world responded, "compassion fatigue" unveiled as the straw man of cynics and ad salesmen. Epic catastrophe was met by epic generosity, without benefit of untapped oil reserves or geopolitical gain. The UN is here in force, but the real united nations are the small NGO's from every corner of the planet who just showed up, flying by the seat of their pants. String their acronyms side by side, and they'd go halfway around the equator. Recite them, and you'd be speaking in tongues.*

There were maybe three categories of NGO's suddenly working as if the earthquake gave them a reason to notice Haiti. The first category is those that were always around. The Red Cross, Catholic Relief, Doctors Without Borders, World Vision, etc, as well as the government connected groups such as USAID. These organizations have always been involved in the country because they felt obligated to since it is "the poorest in the Western hemisphere." They decided they probably should try to do something there, but they never carried out their work with any motivation or inspiration towards the Haitian culture and what it could become. They just maintained "a presence". These sorts of organizations seemed to welcome the earthquake as a way to provide a little variety to the work that they were doing in the country and as a way to pump in big boosts in funding. These funding boosts meant that as long as they threw some tarps around to justify their relief efforts, then they could use the money for other things and maybe no one would ever notice. It's way too big of a problem to really expect anyone to account for every penny anyway, right? These are the sorts of groups that Zizi and Guy were called to aid as part of the Haitian Scouts in Jacmel and they experienced firsthand the results of the large organizations' insincerity.

The second category of NGO's are all of those foreign groups that always thought of Haiti as just some sort of humanitarian fairy tale used to teach the world lessons on poverty or groups that possibly just saw the country as too dangerous and unstable to be involved with. These groups had been doing their "good work" in other countries around the world, countries where that good work is easier to do, but never imagined getting involved in Haiti until the deadliest natural disaster in recent history hit the country. The prospect of how good it would look on their websites and newsletters if they tried to do something for the poor Haitian earthquake victims then excited these organizations. These groups tend to have a mindset developed from their experience in other countries and cultures of "they're all the same". "This is just like Cambodia, or Guatemala, or Sudan." But there was nothing about Haiti after the earthquake that fit into their rigid relief boxes. These organizations came in and were stunned to realize that nothing was working the way it had for them in other places. If these NGO's had asked the ones in the first category for advice, they could have told them what Haiti was like, which is exactly why those in the first category have always decided to not really do anything, because almost nothing seems to work here.

Then there are the groups that didn't previously exist but formed because of the earthquake itself. These include large international efforts, such as the IHRC, founded by Bill Clinton and former Haitian Prime Minister, Jean-Max Bellerive, and Sean Pean's JPHRO, as well as many small local groups that decided to mobilize Haitian citizens in the relief efforts. Some of them have specific missions to work directly on relief for the victims of the January 2012 earthquake, while others have other broader missions but were formed in the wake of the disaster due to the promising potential for support and sympathy. These organizations have struggled to really make a difference in Haitian's lives for different reasons. One reason is because with such a specific mission you have to have a timetable with an end date. From the beginning you have to have a plan to get out of the situation, but the earthquake in Haiti was such a huge overwhelming problem that any significant relief work towards it could not be expected to be accomplished in any set amount of time. Yet these orgs had to do something with the money that they received in the typical time period of relief work, which meant most of it getting wasted. With the smaller groups, they had vague ideas of wanting to help their country but absolutely no experience or qualifications in carrying out the work and absolutely no system of support from the larger organizations to give them any direction. I've been involved in reviewing a lot of these local organization's requests for support and each one of their letters always begins with, "Since the earthquake of January 2010 we have judged it important to...(insert general mission statement here)". So they continue to hold on to their own acronym for help, but never are able to take any steps.

Then there are the extras that don't fit into these categories. There are the mission teams who are perhaps the most entertaining of the swoopers. They come in with their good good hearts dressed like they are going camping or on a safari or to a reunion for some fundamentalist religious cult. Or they come wearing poorly designed, matching t-shirts. No one wants to help more than they do. They've always felt called to do some sort of mission work, or maybe have been hooked on the idea through other training wheel mission trips. They're really good at hugging babies and painting walls and singing "He's got the whole world in his hands" but throw them into the middle of a catastrophe of this scale and it's a whole different ball game. None of them are actually trained to handle such trauma or experienced in even witnessing such overwhelming devastation.

It becomes a competition between jaded cynicism and reckless naivety for which can cause the most damage to an already damaged situation. I say this as someone who has been a part of almost all of these groups at one time or another. I also suggest these judgments with the accompanying admission that I still encourage most of these groups to continue to be involved in Haiti. Although at the moment of their swooping they may seem like a bunch of bumbling buffoons when looked at as a whole, there are always significant moments for the few individuals within the groups that end up understanding something deeper about the culture and who search out ways to get more effectively involved. If it wasn't for the existence of these various groups I would never find the support that I need to do the work that I do here. For every dollar that I am able to put towards an effective, sustainable, community led program, at least a thousand dollars probably had to be wasted first. But if I didn't accept that huge chunk of wasted funds first, my little dollar may never have even been given. It would have been spent on an order of small fries at the drive through window instead.

Sometimes it feels as if the entire world has just blindfolded itself and is haphazardly throwing aid darts at this mystery target called Haiti. Eventually one of those darts is bound to stick, but never hits the bulls eye.

This is how Haiti has become the giant convergent sheet of aid efforts that confounds even the most respected experts in the field. It is in survival mode but still nothing complete. One enormous mess of random unwanted scraps stitched together in a shamefully ugly quilt of good intentions gone bad. It doesn't work because Haitians aren't quilters - they're weavers. Unfortunately, no one's ever empowered them to do the weaving that they see their country needs.

However, no one would ever need a shelter made of convergence sheets if their home wasn't destroyed in the first place. Haiti's home wasn't broken on January 12th, 2010. It was broken long before by the mouths of the world slowly tearing it down. Criticism, doubt, and jealousy had worked against the country with negative words for centuries. Ever since the slaves successfully revolted against the French colonists in 1804 to become the first "black republic" the rest of the world starting using their mouths saying "savages,"

"Neanderthals," "They'll never be able to run the country on their own". Then through years of political and economic turmoil, as foreign countries got involved in Haiti's affairs under the guise of aid, the words may have changed but the message within them and the destruction they cause remains the same. "We know how to do things better," "Here, let us show you how it's done," "Follow our model because we have all the solutions," "We know what's best for you". The verbal abuse continued in all sectors up to the time of the earthquake. Fundraisers said "poorest country," "the least of these," "undeveloped," and "third-world". The government websites said, "violent," "unstable," and "frequent kidnappings". Perhaps the most terrible mouths of all were those of the media which always remained silent without saying a word.

The infrastructure of this country had been so weakened by the mouths that like to break things apart that it never had a chance of withstanding the blow that it took on January 12th. At that point the mouths had already done all the work. God would have never even had to make the tectonic plates collide. A child could have blown that house down easier than blowing out the candles on a birthday cake.

After laying the groundwork for the world's most horrifying disaster with such negative words, trying to patch things up afterwards just seemed like adding insult to injury. You might as well take a knife and stab a guy then give him a Band-aid afterward to put on the wound. *"Bay kou bliye, pote mak sonje,"* the Haitians say in their proverb. "The giver of the blow forgets but the bearer of the scar remembers." The outsiders meddling in Haiti's affairs forget quickly the negative effects of their previous actions, but the Haitians don't forget the pain that they've been through. So the helpers of the world, the problem solvers, they just keep throwing well-intended punches at the already scarred and battered body of *Ayiti Cheri.*

Even now, long after the quake, mouths continue to spout unnecessary assessments at the little country to try to quantify what all went wrong in the relief effort. They think they're words are going to help turn things around but no matter what they say, it just seems to make things worse. Words like "mismanagement of funds," "corrupt leaders," "organizational mess," and "wasted resources," all try to define with language a situation that any Haitian can tell you defies language's limits.

My friend Choumimi, the Port-au-Prince police officer, was very closely involved with all of these relief efforts, both national and external, because of his position. When I talked to him almost two years after the quake, his attitude towards everyone's opinions on the failures of relief was basically, "Why can't they just shut up and let us live? We were better off before and we know what we need." He told me that all of these outsiders trying to fix things or trying to determine why things can't be fixed were acting like doctors trying to treat a patient without ever asking the patient what's wrong. "They've screwed up every chance that we had to ever recover." He told me.

Choumimi gave me a clear example. He said that I could walk into his house and see him sitting at his table with all of the parts to a telephone sitting on the table in front of him. I could see that he clearly needs a telephone, and as chance would have it, I know exactly how to put a phone together from all of those pieces sitting in front of him. But, instead of showing him how to put the phone together, I just go out and buy him a new telephone instead. "What good does that do me?" Choumimi asked emphatically.

The cliché, "Give a man a fish..." may be used in any other situation but Choumimi's parable was purely Haitian and spoke volumes to the current struggles that his country was experiencing. Well-meaning humanitarians who know thoroughly the trappings of creating dependency with top-down charity systems seem to lose their good sense in such a catastrophic emergency. They forget to practice everything that they preach and throw all the rules of sustainable development out the window as they kick into hero mode and bulldoze over a population's right to creating their own solutions.

Haiti had all the resources that it needed at its fingertips to recover on its own. They could have rebuilt their own country. They may have appreciated some advice on how to put all of the pieces together but now they'll never know how. A new country cannot be bought in the street, it must be rebuilt. But because of all of the promises of what billions of dollars could buy, they've lost faith in those resources that they had and been shown that they have no value. And that destruction of faith in one's own self-worth, or collective worth as a country, is much more impossible to rebuild than buildings made of cement.

This isn't all to say that foreigners shouldn't come try to do good things in the country of Haiti. There is a lot to be done and as fellow human beings we all need to carry the load of our brothers and sisters together. We just need to be aware of how we do it as to not make the load heavier. Haiti's back could easily break from the unbearable load of tents, tarps, clothes, and food dumped upon her. But those who come in with understanding, open minds and effective organizational planning, truly do have the potential to help relieve some of the stress that's been put upon this abused little country.

I have to believe this. Otherwise, I had no right in ever being here myself. This is less a justification than it is my opinion based on my last five years of living here. I may not have all of the answers on how to serve the people of Haiti with a cultural awareness and humane sensitivity, but I do believe that part of the answer is communication and seeing life through the other's eyes. So I continue to share the stories from the time of the Grinder. I know how essential the storytelling was in our own emotional recovery here in Haiti. I believe that it must also play a large role in the country's greater recovery as foreigners continue to search for ways to be involved.

ARTWORK BY ASTREL JOSEPH

DISTRACTION THERAPY

When I talked to a friend of mine from the church choir one day and asked what the earthquake did to her she responded, "Ah, the earthquake took my house but it gave me life."

That was the choice that everyone had to make at that time was whether to focus on what they lost or to focus on the life that they still had. I, along with others, chose to see life. I wasn't the only one tired of dwelling. Others in the community began searching for distractions. For a while, all they could talk about was the earthquake. But after so many days of living consumed by such an upsetting event, they began wanting to talk about absolutely anything except the earthquake. They began looking for distractions to keep them from going absolutely crazy.

On the soccer field Kot Pauline they began having futbol matches again for the first time in months. Kot Pauline was located just a five-minute walk south of Julie's house on top of a small plateau. On one side of the field was a steep drop off overlooking the southern mountain range of LaMontagne and the Caribbean just beyond that. On the other side of the field was the bakery. Futbol matches would frequently get interrupted as they would constantly have to send young children after the balls that got kicked over the steep hillside or over the bakery fence. On one corner of the field was a huge old mango tree that had roots growing in such a way as to create a perfect place to sit. It was on these roots that I would frequently go sit and watch the sunset to find inspiration. The rest of the field was clear and flat covered in a rough white gravel that was ruthless on the players' skin as they would fall during competition.

You usually wouldn't be able to find any activity at Kot Pauline that time of year because all of the futbol players would be busy studying. But there was no school left in the country. No learning, no studying, only sitting and talking about how there was nothing. But there was still Kot Pauline and all the athletes had returned and brought the terrain back to life.

This is what the population needed, a reminder of life. Soccer again may not have been anything heroic, but it was alive. Everyone had a choice of either sitting around and talking about everything and everyone that they lost or they could find a distraction to remind them of what they had.

They started playing matches every night. All of my brothers were playing - Berthony, Nicodem, and Sony. Zizi was there along with Dominque and Petuel. And once they started playing, even more started showing up from the city to join them. Police officer, Choumimi came with his cousin, to play for the team too. And once everyone in the community began learning of the activity on the soccer field, they all came out to watch. Eveline Louis and her sisters were there to cheer on the players. Their mother, Simone, who had moved back to the countryside as well, came out to the soccer field to sell candy and peanuts to the spectators. Astrel and Daniel were there with their brothers and their sound equipment to provide the landscape with Haitian rap music. Rodrigue, Jona and Guy; Tigo, Gaby, and Kenson; Majorie and Yvette; everyone was there to get their mind off the Grinder and enjoy some friendly competition.

The entire community reunited after all of the pain and tragedy that they'd been through to find a vehicle to transport them forward in this sport. It was the spirit of the game that made the unity in suffering tangible on a larger scale than the one on one sharing and it was in that unity that hope would appear. This doesn't mean that they forgot about the earthquake and what it had done, but they weren't dwelling on it anymore. They allowed themselves to get lost in the energy of the game. Their stories were still shared, they just weren't all that they were focusing on.

On the radio, stories of survival began to be broadcast as well. For many days after the earthquake a lot of people who were stuck under the rubble were actually using the radio stations as their only hope of making it out. Once phone communication opened up, people began calling into the radio stations from underneath the rubble to let them know that they were trapped and where they were so somebody could try to come and rescue them.

I was sitting with Sony and Kesnel one day listening as a group of students called into the station that we were tuned to. They were trapped inside of their classroom where they had been in class at the time that the quake hit. The rest of the building had collapsed around them and they had no way out. We heard them say that the smell of death coming from the other rooms around them was so overwhelming that they were sure they would soon suffocate from the stench if not die of hunger or thirst.

I sat there thinking how brave that they were to even have held on as long as they had and how hopeful to have even called the radio station. If I was in their situation, I thought, I would be praying for the ceiling above to fall and eliminate me from my suffering. What an incredibly miserable way to go, knowing that there's no hope, just waiting to die. The rubble was so dense and need so widespread that there was no way that rescue teams could get to them all. And these few on the radio represented so many more throughout the city in similar situations.

Kesnel said, "Well can't they find a way to dig themselves out?"

Sony replied, "With what? Their ink pens and notebooks?"

I don't know what ever happened to that group of students. Only those close to them know whether their call to the radio station was successful in saving them or not. Yet each one of us in the country that heard their desperate plea over the airwaves hurt for our brothers and sisters in that moment knowing that they could have been any one of us. We knew that they were us because they were Haitian. If they died, it was a part of each of us that was lost, and if they survived, then it was a part of each of us that triumphed.

Some triumphs were broadcast loud and clear augmenting the hope that we fought to find each day. It was nine days after the quake that we heard on the radio of one family that did actually get rescued but they had spent the first eight days buried beneath it all. A mother and two of her children were stuck inside a room where four other family members had died. They stayed there next to the corpses of their loved ones the whole time clinging to life in hopes of surviving. During the eight days the mother sustained her two children by spitting into their throats so that they wouldn't thirst. On the ninth day rescue teams found them.

No matter how positive the stories were on the radio, they were still all talking about the same thing and Haitians began craving something different. People in the community were complaining that the only stations that they could find that were playing any music at that point were Dominican.

As the children in the community began searching for distractions in their own ways, Sony and Berthony's youngest brother, Joslyn, and a group of his friends noticed the lack of music around and they decided to respond. They formed a band with homemade instruments created from leaky oil jugs, old tin cans, and scraps of wood and metal they'd found in the streets. Then they began marching through those streets sharing their interpretations of songs from popular artists of the Haitian music genre, compas, accompanied by their own primitive beats.

After coming back home after one of their tours around town, Joslyn showed up with a black eye. He wouldn't tell us how he got it but I thought to myself how kind of refreshing it was to see someone injured in an event that had nothing to do with the earthquake, just everyday life of kids being kids. But their impromptu little band kept making music. And the people of the community enjoyed hearing them. It gave them a welcome change of pace from the monotony of the radio stations. By the second week people didn't need to hear any more stories. They all started sounding the same.

What they needed at this time was their music. It's one part of their culture that they could always depend on to help them forget about their problems. It's one part of their culture that they could always take pride in. It's in their music that they can find messages to remind them that pleasure, love, and life can still exist. If there's some music playing it prevents the memories and fears from stewing inside their thoughts. They may not have been in the mood to dance yet when everything was still such a mess, but a little music in the background would have helped to propel their thoughts forward.

At that point, people would have just loved a little music in their own language on any subject. It took a couple months, however, for musicians themselves to begin creating music directly inspired by the earthquake. It was then that a local group first approached me about helping them to write and record a song based on the catastrophe. The group was Prophetie Squad, which Astrel was a part of, along with Daniel Prevot, and a few other brothers and friends. They had written a song called "Pran Kouraj" meaning "Take Courage" and wanted my help in getting it out to the public so that everyone could hear its message of hope. Having slept as a refugee with Astrel and having heard Daniel's frightening stories of what he witnessed in Port-au-Prince, I knew that the motivation for such a song came from deep personal experience.

I had them sing it for me and write out the lyrics so I could know what it was all about and found myself being very encouraged by the substance I found in it. It was a prayer and farewell for those who had been lost in the quake and a song of strength and resilience for those who survived. It reinforced the positive counsel to rejoice that life is not over for those hearing the song and that they now had the ability to take that life into their own hands and make it better. It was an homage to what had passed but an anthem at the same time to what the future could be. I was inspired.

Then as I was listening to them sing through the song, they got to one point where the beat slowed down a little bit and they said to me, "Here's your part."

"Excuse me?"

"Yeah, you know, just something flowery, kind of R&B. Like Michael Jackson." They said.

"You want me to sing with you?"

"Yeah," they said. "It's not just for Haitians, you know." It was a song that was not important just for Haitians but for people all over the world. Because it's not just Haitians that were affected by it. Even if it hit in Haiti, people in countries all over the planet were connected to it somehow or at least heard about it. Within the song there was a message of how important our unity as humans is to help us make it through. "We want you to be a part of it." They told me. "Not just because you're white, but because we think you can sing too."

"So I'm in the church choir," I told them, "I'm no Michael Jackson."

"Just something small. Give it a try at least." They pressured.

I would have been crazy to pass down the opportunity. The powerful message in the song had a beautiful potential to help people cope. I heard that whisper start to push me towards the unrealistic once again for the first time since the quake, "What the hell, go for it."

"Where was my part again?" I asked them.

So we went on and I did sing with them. Then I also helped them get the music recorded, produced, and then out to radio stations so that the public could hear it and hopefully find a little bit of the courage that they were needing for their lives to get back on track.

What I wasn't expecting through the process was how therapeutic is was for myself. I went into it thinking I was going to help create some music for everyone else, but soon realized that I needed the outlet for some of the mess that was still stagnant inside of me.

I had gone through an experience that was horrible, terrifying, upsetting, and tremendously difficult. But it's experiences like that that are also the most inspiring for a creative artist. Weeks ago I had been run over by the most powerful inspiration I had ever known, and ever since that inspiration had been rolling around inside me. I had been digesting it. Now it was time for some expression. That's where I found my relief.

Searching for this subjective concept of relief in an atmosphere where everyone's got their own opinions on it makes it more elusive. Ever since the earthquake, people back in the States were expecting me to provide this to the victims around me. Relief. But who's responsible for determining how to define that concept? Does it mean building houses, and giving out food and tents, and providing medical care? That's how the Red Cross, and the UN, and USAID, the ones with all the money, seemed to be defining it. Or is it possible that it could become something deeper?

By that time I had already received quite a lot of donations towards this abstract notion of earthquake relief from hundreds of people in the US who wanted to help. I knew that the people who gave each one of those dollars had a vision in their minds of what relief meant when they wrote out their checks. They expected their dollars to go towards the construction and the feeding and the treatment. Yet how could I consciously take that money to do those things when I knew from my personal experience that those things would not even begin to relieve any of the trauma that was still wearing away at the population's emotional security?

I had to be at least partially understanding of the desire to build things. After all, the rebuilding process of my own home had been altogether very helpful at rebuilding my confidence. It was a physical representation of an abstract rebuilding process that needed to happen inside me. And, I had to be eternally grateful for all of those foreign donations in helping me rebuild personally because I wasn't budgeted to have to build the house twice. And everyone knows that all of those other organizations that do define relief through bricks and mortar would never choose this white man as one of their beneficiaries. But those organizations did exist to help the Haitians with those base level needs of existence. But who was there to help them live?

It was in the essence of this search to discover a more significant path to relief that the foundation of Living Media International continued to take shape. Even though we had started making plans for what the organization would be long before that fateful day, we weren't officially established until shortly after on February 1st. We were a baby born underneath the rubble and that changed everything. But by keeping our original focus which was on the arts and creativity, we began to form our own definition of what relief was.

We started supporting other musical groups in the community that were making music inspired by the earthquake but about life. These groups included one that had been newly formed by Eveline Louis and her sisters after they returned to Mizak from the capitol. We opened up the opportunity for people to share their stories in a way that assured them that someone else was listening and someone else cared. Almost all of the hundred plus individuals who shared their stories with us would eventually become involved in Living Media's other diverse programs in one way or another. Whether through our classes, our gallery, our Poverty Intervention Team, or other programs still, everyone would find a way to get involved in this long term collective work of art. We began connecting with more visual artists as well who were recounting their own experiences of the disaster through paintings and sculpture. These artists included not only Astrel and my students, but also Pheonix and his friends who witnessed the sea split at Lakou New York as well as others such as the pastor who prayed with us on the tarp that first night, who also was an experienced painter.

All of these efforts were ways to construct lines of communication to get the true stories and first hand perspectives out to a greater audience. Just as any individual artist knows that you need to get that complicated emotional mess out of your inside through whatever medium you use, as a collective culture, the people of Haiti had to get their popular emotional messes outside of their borders so that others knew what they went through.

Astrel Joseph was one of the first visual artists that we worked with. When I originally came to Haiti he was one of my first painting students and one of my most talented. From early on in meeting him I could tell that Astrel was a young man that thought like an artist. He saw the world like an artist and hoped like an artist. Although he had never had any previous training in the arts whatsoever, he just got it.

It was with Astrel that I began working soon after the quake to see what we could create. We got together with a few other of my previous students and new friends and searched for a place that we could paint. I was still homeless and so was my organization. Astrel's uncle had an unused palm leaf shelter in the old market that was being used as a study center by Astrel's cousins and we decided to convert that into our new studio.

For Astrel, the Grinder had unleashed a new sense of creativity within him and his artwork really turned a corner and headed in a different direction. Since I had known him he had always created serene, controlled Haitian landscapes. He would tend toward the typical kind of paintings that a beginning Haitian artist would create. But after the earth shook and mixed everything up, his imagination started to churn more passionately too and a completely different wave of compositions began to flow from him. He no longer controlled the painting with such precision but rather allowed his emotions to appear abstractly onto his canvasses with little restraint. He began telling his stories through color and line and form and the results were ones that an art teacher would always hope for one of their students. It took this catastrophe to release what I had always known was inside of him.

Astrel's own personal story was one worth expressing as immediately after the quake, rumors reached him and his siblings that their mother who was in Port-au-Prince at the time, had died in the quake. They all believed that they had lost their mother until two days later when she showed up at their house after having walked from the capitol by foot just like Rodrigue Badio and so many others. He and his family spent two days in unbearable grief before they realized they were actually some of the lucky ones. Now Astrel began channeling those memories and emotions into combinations of visual shapes that looked themselves almost like rubble pieced together but speaking volumes on the lives beyond the rubble.

Working alongside Astrel in our new studio space was inspiring. The studio was a beautiful and peaceful place to paint, but also being located in an active part of the community we would frequently have visitors pass by to see what these crazy artists were up to. I had been working on my *Statistics* paintings once again, a series of small intimate portraits of Haitian children. One day I had about ten of my *Statistics* paintings sitting out on a wooden bench next to where I was working when one man came in and greeted us. When he came by and looked at my paintings sitting there he said, in a general manner to everybody in the place, "It looks like this is a workshop to create people." Without even looking up from his own canvas, Astrel responded, "Yeah, we're replacing those that we lost a few weeks ago."

This statement gave me a whole new perspective on what these paintings meant to me, and could have meant for others at that time. It's a series that I had started long before the earthquake and continually worked on no matter what other work I was doing. However, the truth is that I had been working on these paintings primarily because they were what had been selling well, and as much as anything at that point, I needed to create things that were going to be able to raise funds to contribute to the recovery effort. I really hadn't spent much time pondering their new context or trying to redefine them at all in reference to this new tragedy that had so heavily redefined my life. To me, I was just continuing a concept that existed long before January 12th, but still held true, although maybe not directly related to the earthquake. Now, Astrel's comment made me rethink all of that.

I called the series "Statistics," but there were more arbitrary statistics and indefinite estimates thrown around on the days following the earthquake than ever before. Statistics that were meant to directly represent the same people and population that my paintings were meant to represent. So many numbers were pulled out of thin air in those days and stuck to a vague concept of so many people that died in anonymity and then were buried in mass graves and burned in undignified piles. These are exactly the people that a series of paintings like this was meant to give faces to, to show their individual beauty as human beings and make them something more than just bodies or victims. So, thinking of these paintings as a way to "replace those that we lost" then made the work even more personal.

There are organizations and websites and supposed experts who have placed "official" numbers on the death toll of this tragedy, because that's what we have to do as humans to try to make such an incomprehensible thing, in the most minimal way possible, comprehensible in our finite minds. But those numbers don't really mean anything.

No one can know the numbers. It's impossible to count. It's useless to try. Those of us who were here and survived what so many did not, we know how many we lost personally, but as a human race, we will never know how many of our brothers and sisters The Grinder stole from us on that day in Haiti.

Even though I knew that the death tolls were still, and always would be, complete guesses in the dark, and I knew that I would never be able to replace them all with my little paintings, I felt whatever I could create would serve as a tribute and a memory. So much destruction consuming our public consciousness, creation seemed the only antidote.

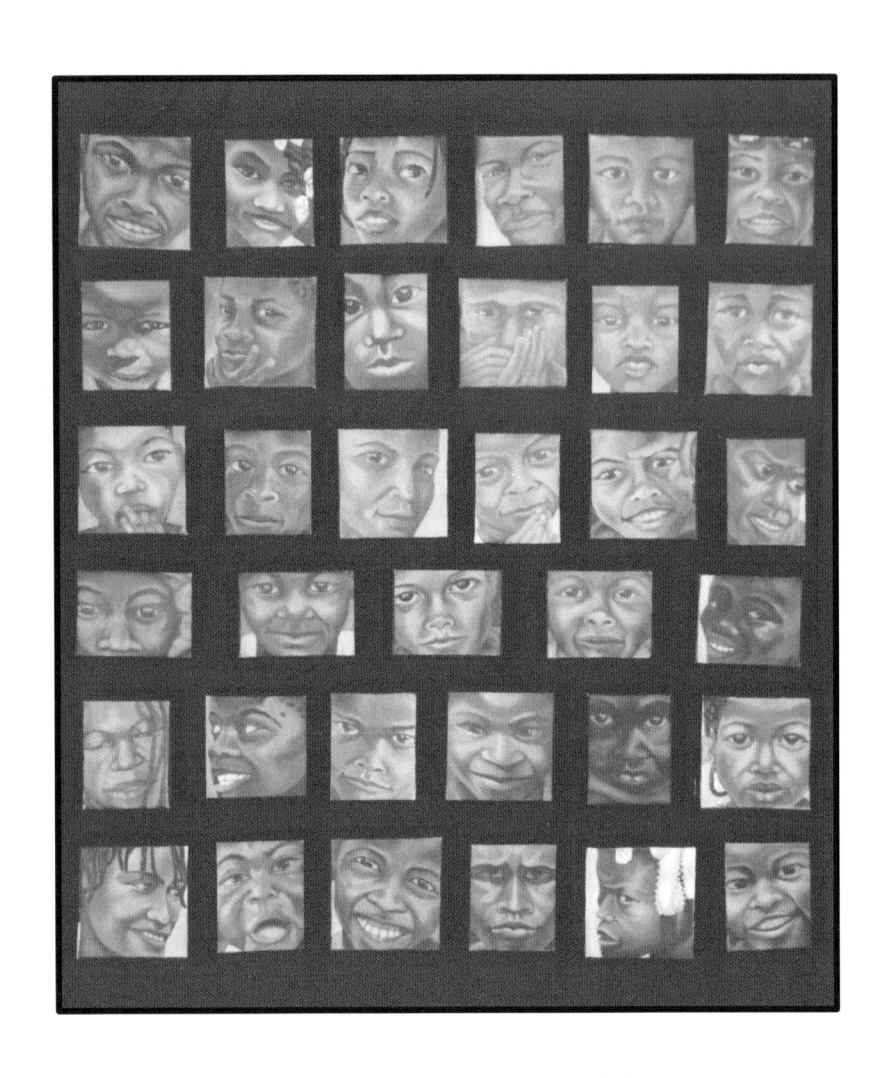

ARTWORK BY LEE RAINBOTH

AFTERSHOCKS IN OUR MINDS

We began the project of collecting people's personal stories within weeks of the quake. We talked to over one hundred people from Mizak and recorded what they lived. And even though I had the inspiration for this book and the intention of making it from the beginning, it took over a year for me to actually arrive at a place where I felt ready to enter into the process of writing it. It took me that long to feel secure enough to revisit the events and memories represented in these stories. And even then, it was a struggle to push through sometimes.

It's the strangest feeling to be so convicted that such a work needs to be created and shared, and yet wanting to completely forget about the entire event at the same time. It's one of those things that as a society we cannot allow ourselves to forget even though for the survivors forgetting may seem like the easiest way to continue living. It may also be easier if the rest of the world just forgets about it, then it also releases them from any responsibility of caring for their fellow human beings who are still struggling with the long term effects of this disaster. Yet, at the time of writing this, I know that much of the world has already done exactly that, forgotten about Haiti and what happened on January 12, 2010.

This is why I did push through and write what I have written. I needed to write something to serve as a reminder as difficult as it may have been for me. There would be times when I would be typing on my laptop and just start bawling to the point of not being able to see my screen. My roommates thought that I was truly crazy at first, but eventually learned, "Oh, Lee's just working on his book again." Those moments proved to me that the process was necessarily cathartic for me.

My roommates, however, understood what I was going through every time that I wrote because they have their own triggers that bring back emotional memories and latent fears. It's actually impossible to live in my house without being confronted daily by reminders of the destruction that occurred that day. Although we have completely rebuilt the house, it is still surrounded by a sea of cement rubble left over from the first house that was destroyed. We walk over that rubble everyday as we step out of our doorways. It has become just another part of the landscape that we barely notice anymore. Yet, subconsciously, we all know exactly what put that rubble there. In the deeper parts of our memories, we still are aware of a time when all people in this country were traversing much larger piles of that same rubble. A time when people were desperate to escape from under that rubble.

Now that some cleanup has taken place throughout the country, an unknowing visitor could possibly have trouble even noticing that an earthquake ever passed through killing hundreds of thousands of people. But to those of us who are acutely aware of every crack in every wall and every morsel of fallen cement, we are unable to take a step without encountering a reminder. There are still the enormous reminders to the entire world that remain evident such as the presidential palace and the Cathedral in Port-au-Prince still lying in shambles. Yet even these icons of Haitian society, after being plastered all over websites, magazines, and newspapers around the world, have become almost cliché landmarks of hopelessness that seem hardly worth noticing anymore.

We don't even need to see something to be thrown back to those unsettling moments. We felt it with every fiber of our being and experienced it with every sense. Now we accept the memories as everyday occurrences. It could be a sound, a feeling, a smell, or just something in the atmosphere that takes us back and makes us weak.

One evening, long after we had moved into my rebuilt house, probably almost a year after the quake, I was sitting out front of the house with Petuel, Papi, and Sony. We were just talking and hanging out but we were sitting on the very rocks where we had laid that evening of the quake amongst our neighbors under the falling stars. I don't know why we chose to sit there that day, but none of us thought anything of it.

We were just relaxing at the end of the day and that happened to be where we landed.

As we were talking Berthony walked up the hill towards us and exchanged greetings but kept right on walking to the house. "Come on over and sit with us a while," we told him. But he looked at us and pressed his lips together tightly as if saying anything would be painful. He shook his head slowly and just turned and entered the house by himself.

The other guys questioned why he was being so unfriendly and just thought he must have been in a bad mood that day, but as I put my hand down on the rough rock that I was sitting on, I realized why he didn't want to join us. My mind flashed back to that night and I recalled him trembling next to me there on the ground, unable to speak, just as he was then, months later.

When I went into the house shortly after I knew well enough not to mention anything to him. Talk about school, or soccer, or girls, or anything, just don't say anything about the rocks that we laid on that evening.

I got to know with my good friends which situations were more fragile for them to deal with. For Papi, I knew that I had to be conscious of large trucks passing by in the road when I was with him. He was simply walking in the main road in front of the public school when the earth started trembling that day and the first thing he did was look around to see where the large truck was coming from. Now, if we're ever walking together in the road and a large truck does pass by, the first thing he does is stop to see if the ground is quaking. All of our instincts have changed.

Kenson, who gave Berthony and I a ride back from Jacmel that first time we went to the city, is still one of my most frequented drivers. I take that route with him from Mizak to Jacmel and back at least once a week, and 9 times out of 10 he still mentions the huge rock at Nan Midi as we drive by. If there's ever anyone new on the moto with us, you can guarantee that he'll point it out. "That's where I was when the earthquake hit," he'll say. "That's where I hid from whatever was going to happen."

Kenson makes a living driving his motorcycle on that road and has to pass by that spot multiple times every day, each time remembering the fear and uncertainty of January 12th. Sharing that memory with anyone who's on the moto behind him brings others into the common experience and ties us together as human beings. Kenson tells his moto passengers. I've written a book for whoever will read. We're all still searching to make the load lighter.

Even now, as I write this almost two years later, the events of that day still come up in casual conversation with my Haitian friends. Just recently I was sitting with some friends at my home in our front room and we tumbled unintentionally upon the topic. Tigo was there along with Kenson, Berthony, and some others. The word "earthquake" originally came up in the conversation as a joke, "Sure, we'll go to the beach next week, as long as there's no earthquake before then." When Haitians used to talk about the future plans they would follow their statement with, "If God wants." Now "If God wants" has become, "As long as there's no earthquake."

As we were talking I noticed Tigo drift away from the conversation and stare upward. "What's up, Tigo?" I asked.

Everyone got quiet and Tigo paused, still looking at the cement ceiling above him, and then he said very seriously, "I'm still not sure that it's not going to fall on me." In my mind I thought, we could go outside and chat instead, but then where would we sit? On the rocks that are too difficult for Berthony to revisit?

Anymore these memories don't cripple us. They're just small daily blips on the radar that exist to interrupt our momentum, but we're able to live normal lives.

For myself, what haunts my memory the most is the smell that I encountered that day in Jacmel. The stench of death from hundreds of bodies filling the air and assaulting your lungs and your confidence is unforgettable. You can close your eyes to the rubble and choose to not listen to the cries but that aroma penetrates your very being and lingers in your soul forever. And to realize that the smell is coming from other human beings that were once living just like yourself, that is the most hellish realization anyone can experience. The scent carries with it a guilt for living.

When I talked to Choumimi, it was this odor of death that he actually credited for the deterioration of Haitian unity in the weeks following the quake. "As the stench began to fill the streets, the solidarity of the people dissipated." It was that something strangely wonderful that I experienced on the tarp that first night that couldn't survive the rancid fragrance of so many brothers and sisters lost. "At 5:10 on January 12th there was neither security nor insecurity," Choumimi said, "only waiting for when the next aftershock would hit." But in a few days that all changed. He pointed out that it was when the city began smelling so bad that people began to leave their homes and their businesses because they couldn't breathe the air anymore that crime started breaking out. That's when the robberies and the violence began, when the stench filled the streets.

It's a stench that has the power to make an entire nation crazy. I only inhaled it for a few short moments and it traumatized me. For those who had to live with it for days before they surrendered and escaped to fresher air, the long-term effects of the smell must be magnified to a horrifying extent.

On another night in my house when Papi, Berthony, and I had already laid down in bed for the night, before any of us fell asleep, Berthony said, "You guys smell that?" We all had smelled what he smelled, but I guess we weren't going to say anything since we were already comfortable in our beds. "There must be something dead in the room."

"We'll find it in the morning." Papi said (he never went to the city when the stench of death consumed the air).

"No, it's not like you just forgot to wash your feet, Papi, something really stinks." Berthony continued.

I got up, turned on my flashlight, and started sniffing to find where the smell was coming from. The other two followed suit and we all ended up deciding that the odor's origin was somewhere at the foot of Berthony's bed. We began taking everything off of the shelves that were there and looked under the bed and in the corners and crannies there with our flashlights but didn't find anything. As we moved everything around the smell only got worse. We all searched for t-shirts or handkerchiefs to tie around our noses and mouths. We lifted up the mattress and box spring, still nothing, but the stench was definitely coming from the area. I sniffed the box spring closer. "I think it's inside." I told the guys. We ripped the bottom covering off of the box spring and looked inside. We still found nothing.

By this time the bedroom itself looked like an earthquake had passed by with everything strung all over the floor and the three of us starting to look like wild men on a fanatic rampage to uncover the culprit of this smell. We had removed everything from that side of the room and didn't see where else to even look anymore. All that remained were the four cinder blocks that Berthony's bed had been sitting on. We were getting tired and very discouraged. It began to seem the only way to get rid of the smell might be to burn the house down.

Then Berthony went and pulled one of the cinder blocks out from next to the wall, and there, stuck between the block and the wall was the carcass of a small rat. When he pulled the block out, an even stronger whiff hit Berthony and he jumped back, "Oh God! That's mean!" There was the victim, squished in between the cement block and my cement wall. The rat must have been crawling along the wall behind the block at just the right moment when Berthony shifted his weight on the bed and crushed him. A death caused by two layers of concrete colliding causing a stench that I never wanted to smell again in my life. It was just a rat, but it was enough to bring back far too many memories that we weren't planning on remembering at that moment.

Papi put a plastic sack on his hand and took care of the body. Berthony went to get some water and floor cleaner and I took the block and threw it outside. We scrubbed down the entire area with water, floor cleaner, and shampoo, but it still stunk. We doused it in hand sanitizer. The stench was still too much to sustain. We opened up all the windows but couldn't stay inside. We all went out on to the porch for some fresh air.

We removed whatever we had tied to our faces and took in deep breaths of the fresh night mountain air.

"It smells like Jacmel after the quake in there." Berthony said.

"I know," I responded. "I don't think I can go back in there."

Papi stood up and said, "Wait for me. I'll be right back."

"Ummm, okay." Berthony and I looked at each other confused and Papi rushed off.

A couple minutes later he came back with a pack of menthol Comme Il Faut cigarettes. He opened the pack and handed us each one. "Come on," he said and went back into the bedroom.

None of us are smokers but at the time it seemed like the best idea of how to get rid of the smell. Back in the room we found a box of matches and lit up. We closed all of the windows back up so that the cigarette smoke would replace the stench of death. As we sat there smoking we joked about how it took a situation like this to ever get us to have a cigarette together. If it was just a smelly rat, we probably would have just let the room air out and have gone to sleep in the other room with the other guys for the night. But we couldn't do that because we knew that the smell lingering in our nasal cavities would cause nightmares. We had to replace the smell with something else and laugh away the memories. The cigarettes were doing the trick. After we each finished one we lit up another, and then another. We sat there smoking and talking until the three of us had finished about half a pack.

By that time we couldn't smell the death anymore, all that we could smell was the nicotine smoke in the air. This was a million times better than the alternative. We found another cinder block outside to replace the one with rat guts on it that we had disposed of and stapled the box spring back together. We tucked the rest of the cigarettes away in case we would need them again in the future to erase any memories. Then we put Berthony's bed back in place and all laid down again for the night still laughing about what we had just gone through.

"People would think we were crazy if they saw us just then!" Berthony said.

"Not if they lived through the earthquake!" Papi responded.

This is how we have moved on with our lives, aware of constant reminders, but never accepting defeat. Now we press on ahead depending on one another to lean on for understanding and camaraderie in the fragile times. We cling to the something strangely wonderful that we still know runs deep in the Haitian spirit. In this country we may not have money or the latest technology or a single drop of infrastructure or any hope in the organizations that control things, but we have each other. Even these days when a tremor rumbles up inside of your spirit, you can always look to the person next to you and know that they understand because they were there. They have their own tremors still rumbling. You know that the moment will come when you will have to support them too. The moment will come when you will have to wipe their tears and hold on to their shaking, scared hands.

I write these final words on the eve of the two year anniversary of The Grinder. I am writing them as I broadcast my evening radio show on the local station here in Mizak. My laptop screen is blurry once again from the tears filling my eyes, unable to remain unshed as the memories flow. The other DJ's sitting in the booth across from me see me tearing up as I pass DeMarco's "I Love My Life" over the sound waves and they simply smile because they understand. They know what tomorrow is and they know who I am.

It's been two years, however, you could be reading this years from now and I'm sure that these comments will still hold true. Those of us that survived to tell what we lived in the earthquake will hold on to these memories until the day that our own stars fall from the sky. Until that time, I continue to look up into the sky and thank God, wherever he may be hiding, that my star is still shining.

A portion of the proceeds from sales of The Grinder will go back to support the programs of Living Media International. For more information, please visit www.livingmedia.org.

ABOUT THE ARTWORK IN THIS BOOK

All of the artwork in this book was created by artists that work with Living Media International and the images are reproduced here with their consent. Rights to the artwork remain that of the artists that created it. To view the images in color and learn more about the artists that created the work, please visit www.thegrinderbook.com/theart.

ACKNOWLEDGEMENTS

Sure I may be the one who typed this book up and crafted it together, but it took the positive energy of many people to make it happen and I am grateful for every last one of them.

First of all to the dozens of survivors who were willing to share their stories with the world. Your strength is an inspiration. To my community of Mizak for accepting me as one of your own and showing me what it means to be human. Especially to my roommates and brothers, foremost Berthony, Papi, and Sony, who make every day here worth waking up for, for sharing your lives with me unconditionally and for naturally being such essential characters for a story like this. To my staff at Living Media, Serge, Jona, Kesnel, Yvette, Roberson, Petuel, and Majorie, for believing in a unique vision for a community and doing all the work to fulfill that vision.

Thank you to my Living Media Board of Directors: Maria Lux, Ellen Kamischke, Brent Olson, Jessica Leavitt, and Terry Pollard for all of your support along the way. Extra thanks to Maria for the technical help on pulling this book together and Ellen for all of the editing, advice, and contacts. To all of those who have inspired and encouraged me along this journey and those who have helped get the work done while I write. Judy Haselhoef, Robert Negron, Angelica Laudermith, Sarah Letsche, Vicki Jay, Desiree Chantal, Audrey Jones, Katie Wilberding-Cross, Jason Storms, and the many more that I cannot name.

To all of the literary agents and publishers who rejected this book, thank you for teaching me so much about the world of writing and helping me along the way to improve the work.

A huge thank you to my incredible family for sticking behind me through it all and especially my parents, Clark and Vickie. Without your love and support, I'd be working at a coffee shop and making bad art on my time off.

And finally to the God among us that somehow keeps pushing me on through it, providing the drumbeat for me to march to in this crazy life I've ended up in. Thank you.

ABOUT THE AUTHOR

Lee Rainboth is a visual artist, nonprofit manager, traveler, and storyteller. He is a cofounder of Living Media International and currently serves as the organization's Executive Director. He lives in Mizak, Haiti where outside of the nonprofit he also sings, writes, and performs with a rap group, Prophetie Squad, and manages a soccer team, L'Union. He is the creator and author of The Green Mango Blog, a site dedicated to thoughts on international service and living based on his experiences in Haiti and elsewhere.

www.thegrinderbook.com
www.livingmedia.org
www.thegreenmangoblog.com
www.leerainbothart.com